A WILD CIVILITY

WITHDRAWN

PATRICK J. KEANE

A WILD CIVILITY

INTERACTIONS IN THE POETRY
AND THOUGHT OF ROBERT GRAVES

A LITERARY FRONTIERS EDITION

UNIVERSITY OF MISSOURI PRESS

COLUMBIA & LONDON, 1980

The time to write this essay and a much longer study of Yeats was made possible by a generous grant from the National Endowment for the Humanities. I owe a special debt of gratitude, as well, to Robert Boyers, editor of *Salmagundi*—and for much more than the reading of the manuscript. Above all, there are the two obvious debts to be acknowledged. To borrow a line from W. H. Auden's posthumously published poem "A Thanksgiving"—"*Yeats* was a help, so was *Graves*."

This book would have been dedicated to my wife, Ann, and my mother, Margaret, were it not for the discourtesy of death.

Copyright © 1980 by
The Curators of the University of Missouri
University of Missouri Press, Columbia, Missouri 65211
Library of Congress Catalog Card Number 79–5428
Printed and bound in the United States of America

Library of Congress Cataloging in Publication Data
Keane, Patrick J
   A wild civility.

   (A Literary frontiers edition)
   1. Graves, Robert, 1895–   —Criticism and inter-
pretation. I. Title.
PR6013.R35Z727   821'.9'12   79–5428
ISBN 0–8262–0296–9

To the Memory of My Father
Joseph Patrick Keane (1911–1979)
whose wild civility combined
exuberant Irish humor with
the courteousness of a
verray parfit gentil knyght

A WILD CIVILITY

I

It has become something of a tradition for those who write about Robert Graves to end their discussions, as George Steiner, W. H. Auden, and Daniel Hoffman do, by quoting Graves's admirable poem "A Plea to Boys and Girls." We might begin with it.

> You learned Lear's *Nonsense Rhymes* by heart, not rote;
> > You learned Pope's *Iliad* by rote, not heart;
> These terms should be distinguished if you quote
> > My verses, children—keep them poles apart—
> And call the man a liar who says I wrote
> > All that I wrote in love, for love of art.

Agreeing with Steiner's judgment that this is "one of the most accomplished short lyrics written in English since Landor," I would add that the accomplishment includes the skillful reworking of old materials: an instance of the grateful receiver bearing a plentiful harvest. The poem begins, ungratefully, by employing the despised Pope against himself—

> Chaucer's worst ribaldry is learned by rote
> And beastly Skelton Heads of Houses quote—

and ends by echoing the adamant monosyllabic denial of Shakespeare's Lysander that his love for Helena is feigned:

> I swear by that which I will lose for thee
> To prove him false that says I love thee not.

In capping epigrammatic (Popean) wit with a splendid (Shakespearean) challenge to be made in his name, Graves improves on both.[1]

As these opening comments are intended to suggest, my approach to Graves's poetry and thought emphasizes two "interactions." The first, illustrated in this poem's fusion of love and love of art, is the poetry's mixture of passion and precision, emotion and artistry: a balance I refer to, borrowing Robert Herrick's familiar phrase, as Graves's "wild civility."

The second interaction has to do with Graves's consciousness of his place in what he called the great "procession" of poets. The echoes in "A Plea to Boys and Girls" are fully conscious. In one of his Clark lectures, delivered about four years before he wrote the poem, Graves cited the Pope lines (slightly misquoting a couplet from one of the Horace "Imitations"), simultaneously dismissing Pope as a false poet and Greek-less "translator" of the *Iliad*.[2] On the other hand, Chaucer, Skelton, and Shakespeare—all "true" poets—are listed among Graves's "masters" in his early twenties poem "In Procession."

The list, given in lines deleted after 1938, includes, along with the above three, Marlowe, Donne, Blake, Shelley, and Keats. Graves's interaction with his predecessors is complicated. Though there is "no jealous eye" among these "poets of old" who, "Each with his pen of gold / Gloriously writing, / Found no need for fighting / In common being so rich," there is a clear sense of tradition and the individual talent and of succession, with each generation "Sinking a new well when the old ran dry." And Graves voices his own visionary "ambition" to "stand at the top rungs / Of a ladder reared in the air." Could he do so, he would be

> The Prince of all Poetry
> With never a peer,
> Seeing my way so clear
> To unveil mystery.

But the poem ends (the coda, like the preamble, was later cut) in a relapse from this "Marvellous hope of achievement / And deeds of ample scope," with the "deceiving and bereavement / Of this same hope." He regresses: "back to the sweets / Of Spenser and Keats," just as the ambitious young Keats before him had taken temporary refuge from the more profound demands of his vision by luxuriating in Spenserian romance.[3]

Graves's *Collected Poems* is a record of achievement and a falling-short of the heights attained by his great predecessors, particularly those in the Romantic tradition. In the present study, there has been no attempt, especially given the shortness of the book, to engage in a systematic assessment of the whole spectrum of Graves's verse—a wide parish that, in terms of types, includes, along with all the love poems, recollections of childhood and of war; psychological studies and more detached "observations"; landscapes, no less psychological; satires, grotesques, epigrams. In terms of phases, the poetry ranges from the early war-haunted lyrics through the more analytical work of the midtwenties and the rich, resilient poems of the Laura Riding period, to the powerful White Goddess poems and those added since 1959, a year that saw the emergence of the White Goddess's more benign Black sister, under whose Sufic aegis the old Graves has written hundreds of lapidary poems marked less by emotional conflict than by what he calls a "miraculous certitude in love" (*OP*, p. 445).

Leaving aside for the moment this more recent body of work, a systematic assessment of Graves's poetry would merely duplicate a task already admirably accomplished by Douglas Day, whose book was published in 1963, and Michael Kirkham, who takes the story through the publication of the 1965 *Collected Poems*. Nor is it really necessary to supplement their work, the value of which is hardly affected by the poetry Graves has published since. Indeed, the post-1965 work—though its nearly three hundred lyrics constitute fully 40 percent of the poems Graves has chosen as his final canon—seems likely to diminish rather than enhance his reputation. For that reason, and because Graves has over the years deleted, along with the weak, some of his strongest poems ("Saint," "Recalling War," and "The Destroyers" among them), I for one am unwilling to accept *New Collected Poems* as the definitive record of Graves's accomplishment.

In a number of ways the situation has altered since the midsixties. At the time, Graves was, however belatedly, very much "in." He held the Chair of Poetry at Oxford, an unusual pulpit for this most iconoclastic and anti-Apollonian of poet-critics, and he had been enthusiastically taken up by the

"Movement" poets in England. Today, a decade and a half later, Graves is even more a household word; but as an old soldier and scholar of Roman history, he may have been reminded, especially over the past five years, of the triumphs of ancient Rome. In those processions celebrating the return of a victorious general, a man shared the chariot of the hero, whispering in his ear of mortality and of the transience of earthly glory. A similarly subdued note attends the triumph of Graves. His international fame, first achieved with *Good-Bye to All That* (1929), has never been greater. It is still riding the crest of the superb television dramatization of the Claudius novels, books that seem to have been translated into every language on earth; and a major film, starring Alan Bates and Susannah York, has been made of his remarkable 1926 short story, "The Shout." But the publication of the "definitive" collection of his poems, virtually certain to be the last collected volume that will appear in his lifetime, has gone almost unnoticed.

The irony is that, for almost half a century now, Graves has been insisting that his prose is merely the day labor of a poet hymning his Goddess by the raging moon.[4] It is on the poetry that he takes his stand and as a poet that he wants to be judged and to be remembered in the history of English literature. Thomas Hardy, whose poetry has always been admired by Graves, insisted that *his* novels too were secondary to the poetry, a conviction largely, and I think correctly, vindicated by modern criticism. What about Graves?

One of the difficulties facing any judgment of Graves's poetry is bibliographical. Since 1926, Graves has put into practice his belief that a poet must revise, and so revive, his canon every few years. It is an act of ruthlessness and of "social politeness" for a poet to "cut his canon down to a reasonable size." Had all his predecessors shown "decent testamentary politeness," he told Oxford University students in the sixties, their required reading list "would be wholesomely curtailed." The alternative is to invite the "old-clothes-men of literature" to make a final judgment that properly belongs only to the poet (*OP*, pp. 594–96, 120–21).

4

Graves's final testament is *New Collected Poems*. The English writer John Wain, who visited Deyá in early 1979, reports that for Graves, now in his mideighties, "the long struggle to write well is over. His life, these days, is a rest from all that arduous, honorable toil."[5] Though *New Collected Poems* is unmistakably intended by the poet to supersede not only the earlier individual volumes (of which there are more than fifty) but the preceding seven collections as well, it is doubtful that any one volume—other than the variorum edition of the poems of Robert Graves, tentatively under way and based on the variorum edition of Yeats—should have canonical status.[6]

This is especially true given what seems to me Graves's disservice to his own accomplishment: his overvaluation of the work of the past decade and a half in relation to his poetry as a whole. The late poetry has not lacked defenders. But while some have found it as fine as anything Graves has written, only a minute fraction of it seems to me to approach the level of his best work. Though this post-1965 poetry bulks large in the canon (160 of the 403 pages, or sections XIX–XXX, of *New Collected Poems*), and though Graves is insistent that a poet should establish his own final testament, my emphasis falls on earlier poems demonstrating Graves's true virtues, with the main themes of this book being indicated in its unwieldy title.

The "sweet disorder" that "bewitches" Robert Herrick in the poem that supplies the main title is really an artfully arranged appearance of disarray; the chaos remains organized, the wildness reined in by a civility reflected in the neatly turned couplets of "Delight in Disorder." For all his anti-Apollonian emphasis on the "supralogical element" in poetry, Graves's poetic "unreason" is no more chaotic than Herrick's disorder.[7] Even after his attraction to the irrational and mythical was solemnized in his official bewitchment by the White Goddess, that allegiance did not preclude intelligible communication: the lucidity and almost-Horatian impassioned plainness that mark Graves's work in both poetry and prose.[8] Who else but Graves could be praised by both John

Crowe Ransom (as a British traditionalist who, like Yeats and Hardy, performed with ease within prosodic restraints) and by Karl Shapiro (as a man whose relationship with the White Goddess makes him—like such other "Romantics" as Henry Miller, Whitman, Jung, Ouspensky, and Reich—an occult poet of "cosmic consciousness")?[9]

The poetry represents a marriage of craftsmanship with fearful and loving worship of the Muse; and both partners are exacting. In responding to that poetry we should be guided by its disciplined intensity, the reflection of a temperament that makes Graves at once a poet of ecstasy and unreason and a commonsensical rationalist who dreads excess and whose versecraft is always meticulous. Denis Donoghue, reexamining T. S. Eliot's speculations about what makes a poet minor, observed in 1978,

> To be a minor poet today is not a sign that the poet has failed in a great ambition to be a major poet: It may just as convincingly mean that a poet has turned back, in horror or in irony, from the occult demands usually and desperately glossed in terms of genius, mystery and madness.[10]

Graves—who, as we shall see, insists that he writes "minor" poetry—seems to have submitted to the occult demands and, simultaneously, to have kept his sanity by maintaining a poised balance compounded of horror and irony.

A balance or a marriage requires two elements. Though the duality in Graves was certainly reinforced by the postwar effort to retain sanity after exposure to the cosmic unreason of the trenches, it would seem to be rooted in his biological and poetic heritages. He makes much of the difference between the precise, puzzle-solving Graveses and the generous-hearted but imperious von Rankes; his mother, to whom he claims he owes so much as a writer, combined gemütlichkeit with command. He has also insisted that his poems, which are certainly in the Romantic tradition, have at the same time remained "true to the Anglo-Irish tradition into which I was born." That legacy is reflected in his humor, his mixture of passion and precision, his pedantic extravagance and skeptical wit: it is less surprising than fitting that Graves should be included in the recent *Book of Irish Verse* edited by the Irish poet John Montague.

The Anglo-Irish strain in Graves may, in turn, help to explain his paradoxical relationship, both intimate and tenuous, to visionary Romanticism. While the great nineteenth-century Romantics maintained an imaginative balance that was more than rational without being irrational, some of their twentieth-century followers have been tempted to yield themselves up to the occult. Graves's version of Yeats's *A Vision* and D. H. Lawrence's *Fantasia of the Unconscious* is, of course, his "Historical Grammar of Poetic Myth," *The White Goddess*. But whatever his attraction to the mysteries and primitivistic rites surrounding that fatal Muse, Graves has a post-Renaissance mind and a passionately skeptical Anglo-Irish temperament that combine to keep his magical-shamanistic tendencies in balance.

Graves's wildness takes the form, then, of a wild civility. Though, necessarily, I deal with Graves's myth of the White Goddess (and, briefly, with Laura Riding, his incarnate goddess during the dozen years prior to World War II), I am primarily concerned with the sophisticated double-mindedness that allows Graves to check emotional commitment with urbane skepticism, to be both the passionate devotee and the erudite scholar of the Muse he worships. Sensitivity to that duality brings us close to what the poems actually do and say. For related reasons, I include an analysis of this double-mindedness as it appears in Graves's major mythographic work, *The White Goddess*.

*   *   *   *   *

"Interaction" begins with the two sides of Graves himself—and opens out. The Romantic and Anglo-Irish traditions have already been mentioned. I am interested in Graves's participation in both; and we will come shortly to his relationship to the colossus bestriding these two traditions in modern poetry. What I mean by this more encompassing interaction can best be explained in terms of my response to the major critical examinations of Graves's poetry. Though there were important early studies—the pioneering essays by G. S. Fraser and Randall Jarrell, the British Council pamphlet by Martin Seymour-Smith, the short book by J. M. Cohen, the appreciation by George Steiner, and the critical essay by Ronald Gaskell—the crucial books are those of Douglas Day, Michael Kirkham, and Daniel Hoffman.[11]

One of the few criticisms of Day's *Swifter than Reason* (1963) was that it might have been an even "more valuable contribution" had Day "given himself completely to a discussion of the interrelationship between Graves's poems and the tradition in which they are written."[12] Kirkham's penetrating study—*The Poetry of Robert Graves*, completed in 1966 and published three years later—consists for the most part of intrinsic analyses of individual poems. The book is canonical in approach in that it demonstrates a thorough knowledge of the whole Gravesian corpus; but the larger canon—the tradition in which Graves has written his poems—is somewhat distorted by Kirkham's New Critical contrast between realism and romanticism, the latter usually synonymous with the outmoded, the illusory, the naive. This is a helpful approach to understanding Graves's middle phases, but it is finally reductive, Romanticism being too complex a phenomenon to be defined, let alone dismissed.

One advantage of the splendid—and, in every sense, central—Graves chapters of Hoffman's *Barbarous Knowledge* (1967) is that the book's wider scope establishes a Romantic-mythical context that permits comparison of Graves's work with Yeats's and, to a lesser extent, Edwin Muir's. Hoffman's greater freedom (though enthusiastic, he is not a Gravesian taking the poet at his own valuation), his greater imaginative range, and his greater range of reference are the fruits of this comparative approach. The appeal of Graves's poems, particularly of his mythical poems, is enhanced and widened, it seems to me, to the extent that they can be shown as related, not only to Graves's own myth, but also to the larger literary tradition. It is, again, a question of tradition and the individual talent. It may be true, as Hoffman says, that "like Yeats [Graves] does not really need to be monumentalized by a scaffolding of scholarship for the reader who is alert to his primary meanings and has enough empathy to imagine the elaborations they suggest" (p. 217). But the slight reservation implicit in that "really" extends Hoffman's observation in the sentence immediately preceding: "Although all readers of Eliot accept the notion that a poetry of allusion incorporates the original contexts into its own texture, Graves has not, so far as I know, been much read in this way." That kind of reading, though less than indispensable, can surely anchor and enrich the imagined elaborations. I am, for instance, increasingly persuaded that Graves's *is* a poetry of allusion and that at least some of his tonal subtleties can be better appreciated by tracing certain interactions with his literary sources: in the Bible, in Shakespeare, in Spenser, in the Romantics.

The inevitable interaction, and the most instructive, is that with Yeats—another poet who maintains a taut balance between wildness and civility and a mythographer who has traveled, with rather less anthropological learning than Graves, through strange seas of thought to piece fragments into a whole, thus clarifying vision and providing metaphors for poetry. The connection between Graves and Yeats, frequently touched on but never really explored, goes well beyond their dual heritage, Romantic and Anglo-Irish. Both have created mythographic systems to provide a wider and more coherent framework for their poems; both are attracted to cyclicism; both submit themselves to a barbaric Muse, a femme fatale with lunar affiliations. Above all, both locate their central and obsessive theme in the human sexual relation of man and woman; and few would dispute that they are the two major love poets writing in English in this century.

Yet Graves consistently denounces Yeats. I therefore take up what has been, from Graves's side at least, an embattled and embittered relationship. This discussion, the fullest on the subject so far, illuminates Graves's otherwise inexplicably violent attacks on Yeats, particularly in the notorious

Clark lectures. More importantly, it can tell us a good deal about Graves's own conception of his path as a poet—a path shadowed, for all his protestations, by what he himself called the "Yeatsian Spectre."

The most obvious difference between the two is that Yeats is an indisputably "major" figure, while Graves—as he himself not only admits but insists—is a "minor" poet. With his characteristically oxymoronic mixture of arrogance and a sense of limitation, Graves ranks "good" or "minor" poets above "great" or "major" poets. But beyond this categorical legerdemain there is a serious, and poignantly human, issue. What impels a man to dedicate a long life to the making of minor poetry—especially when the man is a writer who has produced so immense a body of work, mythographic and poetic? The situation lends credence to the observation (by one of the editors of the 1973 *Oxford Anthology of English Literature*) that Graves is "a poet whose major poetic work may not be in his poems at all, but rather in a strange, disparate corpus of mythographic writings in various forms," and that without that larger corpus, on its own, Graves's verse might have "fewer claims to major importance." Establishing a poet's "major" or "minor" status in the procession of bards is a matter, at its most vulgar, of the rising and falling stocks of fashion, and Graves has nothing but contempt for artists who strive to out-zeitgeist the zeitgeist. Even at best, ranking seems a dubious exercise extrinsic to the poetry. And yet the peculiar case of Graves demands that the issue be addressed; I try to in the final section.

From my own experience, Graves emerges as what W. H. Auden called him almost twenty years ago: a "poet of honor," a craftsman who has respect for his tools, a man who has often succeeded in transforming his experience of love into art. In that same essay ("A Poet of Honor," in the *Shenandoah* symposium), Auden remarked, "The kind of critic who regards authors as an opportunity for displaying his own brilliance and ingenuity will find Mr. Graves a poor subject." I am less certain than Auden and Hoffman were that Graves has provided all his own glosses and demands

10

no outside scholarship of his readers; but the dilemma Auden said faced the would-be-ingenious critic of Graves has the advantage of allowing us to relish the brilliance and ingenuity of Graves himself. For finding this poet a "poor subject" is a *critic's* problem—one that, happily, does not extend to the reader of the best of Graves's poems.

Finally: if, in the ardor of pursuing interactions, I have occasionally gone beyond what can be proved to the skeptical, I plead the example of audacious Graves himself, who, though an advocate of measure and good sense, has in his historical fiction and mythographic scholarship been speculative even to foolhardiness. The author of *The White Goddess*, *King Jesus*, and *The Greek Myths* clearly agrees with Blake that the road of excess can lead to the palace of wisdom and that prudence is a rich ugly old maid courted by incapacity.

II

It would also be to emulate Graves, who prides himself (and not only in the three books just mentioned) on ferreting out the concealed truth from the received versions of texts, to turn to those poems he has truncated, revised, or deleted from his official canon in order to discover his true relation to his precursors in the Romantic tradition. We have done just that in temporarily "restoring" the canceled lines of "In Procession," and we shall do so again with other poems. First, however, there are earlier, other-than-Romantic precursor-texts reflected in poems retained in the canon. The Bible and Shakespeare are predictable influences. For the first, one instance among many, the sixties poem "She Is No Liar," will have to suffice:

> She is no liar, yet she will wash away
> Honey from her lips, blood from her shadowy hand,
> And, dressed at dawn in clean white robes will say,
> Trusting the ignorant world to understand:
> "Such things no longer are; this is today."

Though successful on its own, this short exercise in sardonic irony is enriched by our awareness of the biblical text Graves is echoing: "Such is the way of an adulterous woman; she eateth and wipeth her mouth, and saith, I have done no wickedness" (Prov. 30:20). It is up to us to decide whether Graves, in accommodating grim Proverbs to his more ambiguous Goddess-theme, is transcribing or transvaluing; but his "source" is unmistakable.

The Shakespearean interactions in Graves are numerous. There are, at the most local level, countless echoes—including the phrase from "Under the Olives" that provided the title of *Swifter than Reason*, though Douglas Day does not note the similarity to Enobarbus's "If swift thought break it [my heart] not, a swifter mean / Shall outstrike thought" (*Antony and Cleopatra*, 4. 6. 34–36). Graves writes: "We never would have loved had love not struck / Swifter than reason, and despite reason." Despite the different situations, both passages center on struck hearts, and the verbal similarity is itself "striking."

Two celebrated grotesques, "Down, Wanton, Down!" and "Nature's Lineaments," derive their titles from Shakespeare plays. More importantly, the deeper meaning of both poems is illuminated by their creative interaction with these plays, *King Lear* and *As You Like It* respectively.

The jocular tone of the priapic tour de force "Down, Wanton, Down!" does not invalidate its serious, and quintessentially Gravesian, theme: which involves not only the subordination of crude, untamed lust to "Love" and "Beauty," but also the need for what Graves calls "the restless and arbitrary male will" to submit to, rather than attempt to "dethrone," the female as Goddess.[13] Graves's levity in the poem can hardly be missed; what has to be emphasized is that for all its punning wit the poem is making a point about overreaching male lust which is as deadly serious as Lear's revulsion regarding female lust: "But to the girdle do the gods inherit, / Beneath is all the fiend's" (4. 6. 123–24).

It is in response to Lear's earlier above–beneath contrast ("O me, my heart, my rising heart! But down!") that the Fool responds, "Cry to it, nuncle, as the cockney did to the eels when she put 'em 'i th' paste alive. She knapped 'em 'o th' coxcombs with a stick and cried, 'Down, wantons, down!' " (2. 4. 116–19). At this point in the play, Lear, having subordinated himself to two women rather less refined than Graves's personified Love and Beauty, is struggling to hold down the madness rising in him. Moments earlier, he had cried out for hysteria to retain its proper place in the hierarchy: "O, how this mother swells up toward my heart! / Hysterica passio, down, thou climbing sorrow; / Thy element's below" (2. 4. 54–56). The title of Graves's poem, in which the poet tells his own risen sexual organ "thy element's below," fuses Lear's dread of the loss of rational control with the Fool's report of what the inexperienced cockney piemaker cried to the frisky and phallic eels.

Lear's self-division takes the form of a conflict between proper order and rising chaos, which ultimately becomes identified with the "riotous appetite" of bestial lust (4. 6. 122). The tone of "Down, Wanton, Down!," adding exuberance, humor, indignation, and affection to the serious thematic statement, helps (to use Cordelia's language) to cure the great breach in Graves's own dualistic nature. The poem's persistent questions, combining genuine uncertainty with comic indignation, and the euphemistic terms in which the impudent upstart is admonished—"wanton," "Poor bombard-captain,"[14] "my witless"—reveal a tone compounded of contempt and pity, rude dismissal and affection. The insistence upon hierarchy and decorum, mixed with simultaneous masculine and regimental pride in, dread of, and sympathy for, the intractable phallic force threatening insurrection, provides another instance of Graves's wild civility.

"Nature's Lineaments," borrowing its titular phrase from Rosalind (1. 2. 40), goes on to rudely dismiss nature from the perspective of a Jaques, an *idiotes*-perspective requiring a corrective lens—which is also supplied by *As You Like It*.

"You find," we are told, that all cretinous Nature has

> of mind
> Is wind,
> Retching among the empty spaces,
> Ruffling the idiot grasses,
> The sheeps' fleeces.

It is a nature signifying nothing, a vacuum whose bestial-infantile "pleasures" are "excreting, poking, / Havocking and sucking, / Sleepy licking";

> Whose griefs are melancholy,
> Whose flowers are oafish,
> Whose waters, silly,
> Whose birds, raffish,
> Whose fish, fish.

Shakespeare's banished Duke could find "tongues in trees, books in the running brooks, / Sermons in stones, and good in everything" (2. 1. 16–17); the Gravesian speaker finds *bad* in everything, last scene of all the "fish, fish" clincher, as flat, reductive, and repetitive as Touchstone's "And so, from hour to hour, we ripe and ripe, / And then, from hour to hour, we rot and rot" (2. 7. 25–27). But Touchstone's *sententiae* on time caricature Jaques's tone and style, epitomized in the Seven Ages of Man speech, which is itself a caricature of human life. (Significantly, both speeches are clearly echoed in "Time," the poem immediately following "Nature's Lineaments," which follows "Down, Wanton, Down!," in the *Collected Poems*.) Similarly, the minimalist sketch in "Nature's Lineaments" is identified from the outset as a "Caricature" of the human face. Beyond that caricature—for "Such scribblings have no grace / Nor peace"—are what Blake calls the "lineaments" of gratified human, as opposed to bestial, desire. Unlike the sour Jaques and the biologically reductive Touchstone, both of whom confuse the bestial with the human, Graves, like "Love" in "Down, Wanton, Down!," "Knows what is man and what mere beast." He is therefore capable of recognizing the fullness of life as opposed to its caricature—which both reflects and distorts reality.[15]

Rosalind, dismissing morose Jaques, says she would "rather have a fool to make me merry than experience to make me sad." In this poem, experienced Graves plays the fool with his own melancholy (the vehemence of which, if nothing else, he is obviously ridiculing), and so makes his readers less sad than merry. It is typical of Graves's flying-crooked gift that in choosing a final title ("Nature's Lineaments" was first entitled "Landscape") for his least Arcadian poem he should have recalled language from the most Arcadian of Shakespeare's comedies of the green world. Not, of course, that there is any dearth of satire in *As You Like It*. The point is that despite the internal irony provided by Touchstone and Jaques—all that "burlesque . . . to overcome the simple" as Graves said of Touchstone's "disgusting hyperboles,"[16] all that anti-romanticism to complicate the play—the Forest of Arden and the pastoral romanticism it represents emerge intact, as demonstrably indestructible as romantic love in Graves's "Cry Faugh!" Similarly, the cynicism of "Nature's Lineaments" has undone only the more maudlin landscapes of such rustic collections as Graves's *Country Sentiment* (1920), not the vision of "grace" and "peace" that inspires such idyllic dreams.

"It is a common mistake," as Hazlitt observed in *English Comic Writers*, "to suppose that parodies degrade, or imply a stigma on the subject: on the contrary, they in general imply something serious or sacred in the originals." Graves's anti-bucolic parody, a travesty of the nature poem, treats that serious, even sacred, poetic subject in an undignified and jocular manner. It is both low burlesque and a Touchstonian "overcoming" of those simpleminded enough to take its reductionist caricature at face value. Our full response to the poem should be shaped by the very excesses of its travesty of country sentiment. Following Shakespeare, Graves has freed us to mock with a Jaquesian grimace or a biological reductiveness typical of Touchstone (for whom wedlock is pigeons "nibbling") just those things—physical love and a natural world where even the "raffish" birds go to 't—that, in the end, we embrace with our heart. And the embrace is even more affectionate precisely because of the extravagant rudeness of the dismissal. In the final analysis, "Nature's Lineaments" celebrates, by implication, the "grace" and "peace" its caricature omits—a grace and peace and charm epitomized by Rosalind, whose true delights transcend not only the saturnine caricatures of Jaques and the barnyard lusts of Touchstone, but the merely physical "pleasures" (poking, sucking, and so forth) of nature itself. Here, as in "Down, Wanton, Down!," Graves took more than his title from Shakespeare.

Graves's most intriguing interactions are not, however, with Shakespearean drama, but, inevitably, with poetry in the Romantic tradition, a tradition whose ambiguous legacy Graves shares with Yeats, Lawrence, Thomas, Stevens, and a number of other modern poets he has rudely dismissed. His interactions with the earlier Romantics, though obvious in general, are often obscured in their specific details by Graves, a poet who, like most, prefers to cover his tracks. This is what makes the decanonized poems, particularly in cases where truncation or deletion cannot be justified on purely critical grounds, so fascinating an area for speculation.

We have already looked at the original version of "In Procession." The revised and now canonical text of that explicitly master-haunted poem begins with the speaker, "half-way to sleep, / Not yet sunken deep," witnessing a visionary procession, the colored pomps unwinding "With their saints and their dragons / On the scroll of my teeming mind." The second movement opens by echoing the second movement of "Kubla Khan": "Oh, then, when I wake, / Could I courage take / To renew my speech, / Could I. . . ." What Graves, like Coleridge, longs to revive within him are the "delectable" paradises of the Romantic tradition, synopsized here as the heavenly glories "Of the Land of Whipperginny, Of the land where none grows old." But the poem ends in a failure of nerve: "cowardly I tell, / Rather, of the Town of Hell / . . . / Where between sleep and sleep I dwell."

The interactions in this poem are both experiential, the

impingement of Graves's life upon his work, and literary, an illustration of his sense of continuity with his Romantic predecessors. Graves's poetic phases were largely determined by the two major events of his life. The second was his literary and emotional partnership with the American poet and theorist Laura Riding; but the first was his experience of four years of the horrors of trench warfare, unforgettably described in his great autobiography, *Good-bye to All That*. Out of the trauma of "getting caught up in the First World War, which permanently changed my outlook on life,"[17] came the poetry of the first half-dozen volumes, with fey Georgianism yielding to consciously "anodynic" poetry: bucolic and romantic escapism as frankly therapeutic. Trapped in a less than ideal marriage with an artist and feminist, Nancy Nicholson, who soon began to include him "in her universal condemnation of men," Graves was also neurasthenic; still "mentally and nervously organized for war." He tells us that shells used to come bursting on his bed at midnight even though Nancy shared it with him; "strangers in daytime would assume the faces of friends who had been killed" (*Good-bye*, pp. 289, 287).

Out of these hallucinations and nightmares came the best of the early poems. Though less overtly ghost-raddled than "The Haunted House," "Outlaws," "A Frosty Night," "The Pier-Glass," "Down," "The Castle," and others, "In Procession" is of this company. It is also of what Harold Bloom has called the visionary company, the Romantic tradition. For Graves is here not only echoing "Kubla Khan." More significantly, he is playing a variation on a Coleridge poem that also (in late works like "Vacillation" and "The Man and the Echo") haunted Yeats. This is "The Pains of Sleep," in which Coleridge, tortured by a "fiendish crowd" of nightmare shapes, suffers an undeserved but "unfathomable hell within."

"In Procession" is, in effect, an interaction between Graves's and Coleridge's neuroses, as well as an interaction between two Coleridge poems. Graves entangles the paradisal visions of "Kubla Khan" with the nightmare pageant

17

and "hell within" of "The Pains of Sleep": here, the Town of Hell where "between sleep and sleep I dwell." And the later poet knows precisely what he is doing. In its original version, the text we have was, as we've seen, preceded and followed by lines in which Graves sees himself as in procession with his great predecessors. And the procession is not restricted to those specifically named; though the listed "masters" did not include Coleridge, the revised text seems based on two of his poems.

We may trace an interaction of two other Coleridge poems in a lyric not only retained intact in the canon but also one of Graves's indisputable masterpieces: the 1925 epigrammatic poem "Love Without Hope":

> Love without hope, as when the young bird-catcher
> Swept off his tall hat to the Squire's own daughter,
> So let the imprisoned larks escape and fly
> Singing about her head, as she rode by.

This is "minor" poetry only in length, and few poets are capable of saying so much in many times this number of lines. Both impersonal and deeply moving, the quatrain fuses fantasy and poignance in a typically Gravesian celebration of doomed love. By the time he wrote this poem, Graves had been trying for about two years to resolve his "unceasing emotional stress" in what he thought was a deliberately anti-romantic way, increasingly persuaded that poetry was "not a mere mitigation of haunting experiences," but "an exorcism of physical pretensions by self-humbling honesties."[18] This self-discipline and will to truth, crucial in Graves's conception of his work from the Laura Riding period on and a major theme of the present study, emerge in such a poem as "Pure Death," in which death, stripped of its reassuring bourgeois fictions, is revealed as terrifying but standing "at last in his *true* rank and order." "Pure Death" originally ended with a reference to love's "accomplishment," a word later changed to the altogether less fulfilling "acknowledgement." What we have in "Love Without Hope," written in the same year as "Pure Death," is the acknowledgment rather than the accomplishment of love and a superb example of self-humbling honesty. We are not told whether the young bird-catcher lifts his hat without thinking or in full awareness that he is releasing the birds he has spent all morning catching, though the latter seems likelier. Either way, when he circumscribed his secret love's haughty head with that living, singing halo, he liberated the first of Graves's songs certain to live.

"Love Without Hope," though no less quintessentially Gravesian than "Pure Death," plays off two late poems of Coleridge. In effect, it refutes Coleridge's contention (in the 1829 "Love, Hope, and Patience") that "If Hope prostrate lie / Love too will sink and die." Far from acknowledging that the two cannot be separated, or that one must sink without the other, Graves, in the raised hat and released birds, *elevates* love in its very hopelessness. But Graves's more obvious source, as his title suggests, is Coleridge's moving "Work Without Hope." In that poem, too, "birds are on the wing," though the poet, mateless and out of tune with nature, cannot sing. Graves himself, in one of his *Epilogue* essays, cites the poem's final couplet: "Work without Hope draws nectar in a sieve, / And Hope without an object cannot live."[19]

The unattainable "object" of this heartbroken music was a woman, the "Dear Friend" (Sara Hutchinson) to whom Coleridge sent the first draft of "Work Without Hope." From the accompanying letter—reprinted in the standard Oxford edition of Coleridge's poems and not likely to have been missed by an obsessively biographical critic and Muse-hunter like Graves—we learn that, genetically, the poem is even closer to the bird-catcher's love for the Squire's own daughter. Thinking of Jacob and Rachel, Coleridge initially conceived of the poem as the complaint of a lovelorn dependent bound in service to a man whose daughter he loves but who displays "symptoms of Alienation."[20]

Such symptoms, and the sense of bleakness accompanying the acknowledgment rather than the accomplishment of love, inform two other of Graves's finest lyrics of the twenties. They too, far from being deliberately anti-romantic, interact with the Romantics. And, as in the case of "Love

Without Hope," in whose disdainful aristocrat who "rode by" we may glimpse a portent of things to come, these poems also anticipate the imperious female later to be worshiped as the Triple Goddess.

"Love in Barrenness" (1923) presents us with an austere landscape of mountain and barren plain, psychologically rocky acres. But the next and final stanza of the poem shifts to the sublime—specifically, the Wordsworthian sublime. In the most memorable of the epiphanic "spots of time" in *The Prelude*, a bare landscape with "dreary crags" is transformed by the sight of a girl who seems to "force her way / Against the blowing wind." The scene becomes one of *"visionary* dreariness," dominated by the woman, "her garments vexed and tossed / By the strong wind" (Book II: 302–16 [1805]). Here is Graves:

> The North Wind rose: I saw him press
> With lusty force against your dress,
> Moulding your body's inward grace
> And streaming off from your set face;
> So now no longer flesh and blood
> But poised in marble flight you stood.
> O wingless Victory, loved of men,
> Who could withstand your beauty then?

Though both young women are transfigured into a similarly triumphant symbol, Graves's language is more candid. For beneath the terrible beauty of the sublime this is a sexual parable of force, victory, and submission—as well as an "acknowledgment" rather than an "accomplishment" of love. In a variation on the conventional triangle, the virile aggressive wind is observed—almost voyeuristically, surely enviously—by the woman's companion: "I saw him press / With lusty force against your dress." Unlike the passive speaker, the wind is potent and creative, "Moulding" flesh and blood into a sculpted icon, which is both static ("your set face"; "you stood") and simultaneously charged with vital kinetic energy, "poised in marble flight." She is still of the earth, "wingless," yet inaccessible and tautly poised—her full power still under restraint—on the verge of deification.

The final apostrophe, in another adumbration of the White Goddess poems, is that of a suppliant to a more than mortal woman who rewards his abject worship with marmoreal indifference: "O wingless Victory, loved of men, / Who could withstand your beauty then?"

These may be—as Graves will say in "A Love Story," another bleak and wintry poem anticipating those specifically addressed to the Goddess—"Solemnities not easy to withstand." That is certainly the case with Graves. Whatever the guise—whether this wind-molded Victory or the Squire's daughter riding by her subservient worshiper—we seem, even this early, to be in the presence of Graves's Goddess, whose service, though it may be perfect freedom, is certainly perfect, and self-humbling, service.

Graves comes even closer to that lunar Queen in "Full Moon," the first of his emblematic lunar poems and the sole survivor from his 1924 volume *Mock Beggar Hall*. There the moon, "attained to her full height," is a "tyrannous queen" held to be "Sole mover of their fate" by the phantomlike lovers forced, like the "ghostly" wheat in the "sick" fields, to "mute assent in love's defeat." That defeat transforms "sultry night" and "warm earth" into a polar seascape:

> And now warm earth was Arctic sea,
>> Each breath came dagger-keen;
> Two bergs of glinting ice were we,
>> The broad moon sailed between.

The transformation and the ballad meter, alternating tetrameters and trimeters, as well as the opening "And now . . ." and terminal ". . . between," suggest a recollection of Coleridge's *Rime*, at the point where the ship is driven to the pole:

> And now there came both mist and snow,
> And it grew wondrous cold:
> And ice, mast-high, came floating by
> As green as emerald.
>
> And through the drifts the snowy clifts
> Did send a dismal sheen:
> Nor shapes of men nor beasts we ken—
> The ice was all between. (ll. 51–58)

The moon, incidentally, is not (pace Robert Penn Warren's famous essay) always benevolent in *The Ancient Mariner*. Later the dead members of the crew "All fixed on me their stony eyes, / That in the moon did glitter" (ll. 436–37). In Graves's poem, the tyrannous moon divides the lovers, now grown cold and indifferent, illuminating their "glinting" iciness while, in imagery possibly echoing Coleridge and certainly recalling the final stanza of "Love in Barrenness," they "glared as marble statues glare."

*   *   *   *

We shall touch later on Gravesian interactions with Keats and Shelley; and, of course, the Romantic tradition does not end with them. If the fertile tension between rationality and unreason, the submission to an imagination that is yet intellectually disciplined, is characteristic of Romanticism, then Lewis Carroll is among the Victorians carrying on that tradition of wild civility.

Two compelling twenties poems—"Alice" (1926) and "Warning to Children" (1929)—give us, as "The Terraced Valley" (1930) also does, an inside-out dream world clearly indebted to *Wonderland* and *The Looking Glass*. It has recently been said of the *Alice* books that the heroine embodies Carroll's "own sanity" and that the resolution of the ever-threatening madness is "a trial of strength between Alice and unreason." The "dream world"

> is arbitrary, certain of its own reality, uncompromising toward visitants; nightmare is very close, but can be prevented. Alice is the cool head and equable temper that tames chaos. . . . The vagaries of the imagination can be submitted to—one may fall, float, shrink, swell, be lost and found, be threatened with death and crowned as monarch—and yet survive. Always threatening is the possibility that Alice may be abolished or metamorphosed like the dream objects around her; but it is triumphantly averted.[21]

In "Alice," another Gravesian exercise in wild civility, the chaos-tamer defeats madness by drawing a circle wide enough to take unreason in. The poem sets "that prime heroine of our nation, Alice, / Climbing courageously in through the Palace / Of Looking Glass," to find it inhabited by chessboard personages involved in "never-ending tournament." She becomes spectator and then victorious participant:

> six moves only and she'd won her crown—
> A triumph surely! But her greatest feat
> Was rounding these adventures off complete:
> Accepting them, when safe returned again,
> As queer but true.

There is a clearly marked but crossable boundary between the worlds of logic and fantasy, "that lubberland of dream."

> Alice though a child could understand
> That neither did this chance-discovered land
> Make nohow or contrariwise the clean
> Dull round of mid-Victorian routine,
> Nor did Victoria's golden rule extend
> Beyond the glass.

Perceiving this distinction, and the further distinction between analogy and identity, Alice enjoys the best of both partial but equally valid worlds. That enjoyment, reflected in the gaiety of the poem, is the fruit of Alice's adventurousness and of her "uncommon sense."

If England's prime heroine is Gravesian in her double-mindedness, her Looking Glass world is also Gravesian in what Rosemary Dinnage calls its "ambiguities of space, time, and object permanence" and, above all, in its "reversibility." In "Warning to Children," an image-within-image maze resembling Chinese boxes, we are given a wilderness of mirrors "enclosing" a tied parcel. If we "dare" undo the string we find *ourselves* "enclosed," but with the "same brown paper parcel / Still unopened"—at which point the "endless" riddling process repeats itself. "The Terraced Valley" begins with the speaker concentrating on his beloved and so coming "by hazard to a new region" of "Neat outside-inside, neat below-above, / Hermaphrodizing love." The poem ends with the beloved's voice breaking "This trick of time, changing the world about / To once more inside-in and outside-out."

This breaking of the "trick of time" anticipates "Through Nightmare" and the first of the fully fledged White Goddess lyrics, "On Portents"—poems that embody Graves's fundamental belief concerning time, which is that

> all original discoveries and inventions and musical and poetical compositions are the result of proleptic thought—the anticipation, by means of a suspension of time, of a result that could not have been arrived at by inductive reasoning—and of what may be called analeptic thought, the recovery of lost events by the same suspension. (*WG*, p. 343)

This crucial concept is discussed below, in connection with Graves's mythography, his historical fiction, and "On Portents." The interaction of all this with *Through the Looking-Glass* can be best clinched by citing Rosemary Dinnage one last time: "Reversibility, as in the mirror-image or logical operation, is a persistent theme: the ruminations on time of the Mad Hatter's tea party are developed into ideas of reversible time—remembering the future, explaining unwritten poems."

*   *   *   *

As the work of Graves and Yeats testifies, the English Romantic tradition does not end with the nineteenth century; and it begins much earlier. Near the head of the visionary company is Edmund Spenser, with whom Graves interacts in a poem ("Saint," originally entitled "The Beast") that rather confuses the "saints and dragons" inscribed on the scroll of the teeming mind of "In Procession" and that, like that poem, was later truncated (before being dropped altogether). In its revised form, "Saint" begins, ironically, at the terminal point of the typical romance narrative, with the apparent victory of the Knight:

> This Blatant Beast was finally overcome
> And in no secret tourney: wit and fashion
> Flocked out and for compassion
> Wept as the Red Cross Knight pushed the blade home.

But the Beast, out-albatrossing Coleridge's albatross, refuses to stay dead; he rises from the sea, and lime and fire prove equally ineffective.

What makes this Ransomesque ballad poignant as well as ironic is the relationship between the protagonists—who seem as interchangeable as Graves's titles. In the gutter of the city governed by the saintly "good Knight,"

> would the Beast lie
> Praising the Knight for all his valorous deeds:
> "Aye, on those water-meads
> He slew even me. These death-wounds testify."

We can hardly miss the pun on "lie" and the urbane humor of the situation: death wounds displayed in public by the victim as a prosecutor friendly to the murderer. But the irony is not cruel; the Beast, genuinely fond of the alleged conqueror, seems unaware of the incongruity of his posthumous display.

His survival—"over-dead" and loathsomely wounded—is, of course, a scandal—appropriately so, since the Blatant Beast of *The Faerie Queene* is the embodiment of scandal. The city ruled by the Knight is as infected as Oedipus's Thebes, and the tormented Knight himself "a man shamed / And shrunken." To avoid an embarrassing anniversary celebration of his "victory," the Knight retires from his righteous public duties; turning hermit, he goes

> without farewell
> To a far mountain-cell;
> But the Beast followed as his seneschal,
>
> And there drew water for him and hewed wood
> With vacant howling laughter.

Again, the laughter is not consciously sardonic on the part of this Caliban-like majordomo. In fact, in Graves's complete ironic reversal, the Beast is revealed as something of a saint. Himself "Noisome with long decay," he

> Would bawl to pilgrims for a dole of bread
> To feed the sick saint who once vanquished him
> With Spear so stark and grim;
> Would set a pillow of grass beneath his head,
> Would fetch him feverwort from the pool's brim—
> And crept into his grave when he was dead.

The ambiguity of the pronouns (both Saint and Beast are masculine) confirms the ultimate indivisibility of the two—and clarifies the grim irony present from the opening stanza: Graves meant it when he had the Knight push his blade "home." Irony on irony, the poem unifies the warring halves of "the divided human self" (foreword to the 1938 *Collected Poems*, p. xiii); but at a high cost. The unconscious, instinctual life—the id or libido—will not stay down, however we try to subdue, bury, sink, or purge it away. In Graves's beloved *Golden Ass*, Lucius is transformed into the beast symbolic of his folly and lust; but the "spiritual autobiography" of Apuleius goes on to describe his earned restoration to humanity from that debased condition. In keeping with the grisly humor and thoroughgoing irony of "Saint," the bestial and saintly halves of the psyche, sundered during the Knight's life, are joined only in death. As in Eliot's "Prufrock," unification of the surface and buried selves ("I" and "you") comes only with the final, mutual descent, when *"we* drown."

Graves's poem, as first published, began with three stanzas explaining the allegorical function of the Blatant Beast in Spenser's epic. Though Spenser "loathed" the Beast, we are told, he "withheld the stroke" that would finish him. This was "prudence," for "while the Beast lives / The infamy of his ravage is delight," and gives the Red Cross Knight a "forewon laurel of salvation." The Beast killed, on the other hand, "is carrion and a worse / Than carrion." Prudent Spenser was clever enough to avoid killing the Beast: "Therefore to me it falls to write that curse."[22] These three stanzas were rightly judged dispensable; but the opening stanza of the revised version, in which Graves conflates the first and final books of *The Faerie Queene*, and his verbal echoes throughout reveal a dynamic interaction with the text on which he is playing his variation.

In rewriting Spenser, Graves kills the Beast, but not until that creature has literally killed with kindness the "sick saint" whose "stark and grim" spear of puritanical repression has proven ineffectual. If the Beast in Graves's poem represents "evil," it is necessary evil. For the Beast is both an inherent part of man's nature and the thing whose existence presents us with an object to be tamed, a wildness to be civilized, in order to attain the secular equivalent of "salvation." Tamed or civilized; not extirpated. Whereas Spenser's Redcrosse is a "soule-diseasèd knight" when he gives into temptation and only acquires his "saint's name" (George) after undergoing severe penance in the House of Holiness, Graves's Knight is a "sick saint" (a Nietzschean epithet) precisely because he has tried to suppress rather than sublimate his passions—a process Nietzsche calls "castratism."

The reversal of Spenser is reflected in Graves's verbal echoes of the final canto of *The Faerie Queene*. In the struggle with Calidore, Spenser's Blatant Beast reviles the knight with "shamefull infamy" and "many a forgèd lie," yet it is the Beast who "found his force to shrinke." Graves's Beast would "lie" in the gutter, *"Praising* the Knight," yet it is the latter who is "shamed / And shrunken." Though "supprest and tamed" to a "fearefull dog" who followed Calidore "through the land," the original Blatant Beast escapes at the end. Graves's Beast, an unshakable alter ego following the Knight through the land, might be called Fido. He does not escape in the end; instead, he shares the Knight's grave. But though he seems to die at last, Graves's Beast is not definitively slain, as the Dragon was by Redcrosse in Spenser's opening book. Despite the spondaic finality of "pushed the blade home," the psychological split in the Knight and the ambivalence of the people (whose hearts were "doubt and rue" despite the public festivities and "paeans due") caused the creature to rise once, and he may do so again.

I have discussed "Saint" at some length not only because it is among the handful of Graves's most blatant, and most regrettable, decanonizations, but because it illustrates several additional interactions; let us say, three. The first is with Graves's own life. The earlier poems are filled with web-hung spirits, revenants who refuse to stay dead. The autobiographical genesis of those survivals, of the resurrection of this Beast, of the survival of Calvary by Graves's Christ, is surely the poet's survival of his own "death" in combat; for Graves (who in this context likes to pun on his name) is one of the "second-fated" who have "read their own obituaries in *The Times*, / Have heard 'Where, death, thy sting? Where, grave, thy victory?' " and are "forbidden to walk in grave-yards / Lest they scandalize the sexton and his bride."[23] The Beast redivivus also participates in Graves's theme of crude, unsubduable lust, most familiar to us from such celebrated poems as "The Succubus" and the seriously jocular "Down, Wanton, Down!," but in fact at the heart of countless poems reflecting Graves's divided temperament, one torn between affirmation of love and contempt for the body and its "beastliest" appetites ("Leda"). The final interaction, though the three sometimes overlap, is with other bestial poems of Graves markedly similar to those of the most famous of the last Romantics. For the unsubduable Beast of "Saint" seems Yeatsian as well as Spenserian.

Graves's Beast rises from the deep into which he has been cast, "as evident as before / With deep-sea ooze and salty creaking bones." In the narrative poem that first at-tracted Graves to Yeats, a romance synopsized in Graves's sixties poem "The Broken Girth," the sea demon apparently slain by Oisin ("I drave / Through heart and spine; and cast him in the wave") returns to interrupt the festivities every fourth day, a phallic monster "dropping sea-foam . . . and hung with slime" (*The Wanderings of Oisin*, 2. 181–82, 215–17). This creature, in turn, looks forward to the unsubduable beasts of "Nineteen Hundred and Nineteen" and "The Second Coming," Yeats works with which, it seems to me, Graves has been engaged in a sustained creative interaction—in "Vanity" (1925), "Recalling War" (1938), and "The Destroyers" (1947). Though three of Graves's finest poems, only the first has been retained in the canon. "Recall-ing War," easily his strongest poem on the subject, survived until 1965 when, like "Saint," it was dropped. The third poem, "The Destroyers" (discussed below, pp. 57–61), is now preserved as the climax of what was originally the final chapter of *The White Goddess*.

The direct cause of the Beast's resurrection in "Saint" was the ambivalence of the people; in "Vanity," the cause is misplaced confidence. Two unsubduable creatures—dragon and toad—disturb the fragile peace and illusory certitude of innocent domestic lovers whose naive prophecies of joy awaken these ancestral prophesiers of love's defeat:

> Be assured, the Dragon is not dead
> But once more from the pools of peace
> Shall rear his fabulous green head.
>
> The flowers of innocence shall cease
> And like a harp the wind shall roar
> And the clouds shake an angry fleece.
>
> "Here, here is certitude," you swore,
> "Below this lightning-blasted tree.
> Where once it struck, it strikes no more.
>
> "Two lovers in one house agree.
> The roof is tight, the walls unshaken.
> As now, so must it always be."
>
> Such prophecies of joy awaken
> The toad who dreams away the past
> Under your hearth-stone, light-forsaken,
>
> Who knows that certitude at last
> Must melt away in vanity—
> No gate is fast, no door is fast—
>
> That thunder bursts from the blue sky,
> That gardens of the mind fall waste,
> That fountains of the heart run dry.

Even more admirable than the craftsmanship (with closure of the terza rima achieved by obliquely rhyming "waste" with "Past / last / fast"), is the tonal complexity that celebrates and simultaneously mocks the prettified fragility of "pools of peace" and "flowers of innocence," and the fearful symmetry in which these are reversed by equally naturalized abstractions, "gardens of the mind" falling "waste," "fountains of the heart" running "dry."

This same ambivalence of tone and reversal of naive expectations are to be found in "Nineteen Hundred and Nineteen," which Graves had encountered (Yeats's poem was then known as "Thoughts upon the Present State of the

World") shortly before he wrote "Vanity," composed in 1925 and then entitled "Essay on Knowledge."[24] What both poets "know" in their respective meditations is that (to quote Yeats) "ingenious lovely things" that seemed miraculous are *not*, after all, "protected from the circle of the moon / That pitches common things about." Both poets celebrate and simultaneously mock peace and order, innocence and beauty. These are "pretty toys" we had "when young"; the folly lay, says Yeats, in our "fine thought" (shared by the naifs of "Vanity") that these vulnerable things "would out-live all future days"; that, in the secularized religious faith of Graves's lovers, "As now, so must it always be." But, Yeats announces, "Now days are dragon-ridden," just as before "We pieced our thoughts into philosophy / And planned to bring the world under a rule."

In both poems, we are more than assured that the Dragon is not dead; that planned order, whether domestic or international, is subject to the violent eruption from below that shatters the smooth surface of the pools of peace. Graves's prophetic toad

> knows that certitude at last
> Must melt away in vanity—
> No gate is fast, no door is fast—

The Yeatsian equivalent is a human seer:

> He who can read the signs nor sink unmanned
> Into the half-deceit of some intoxicant
> From shallow wits; who knows no work can stand.

Beyond this, there is the recognition, again shared by both poets, that *knowledge* (to quote the operative word of Graves's original title) is, however painful our entrance into the desolation of reality, preferable to the intoxicated, shallow-witted "vanity" that deludes complacent lovers.

Vanity and naiveté provide the theme as well of "Recalling War," a poem that reveals that the "thunder" that "bursts from the blue sky" in "Vanity" is more than meteorological. Dragon and toad are, Coleridge would say, ancestral voices prophesying *war*. "Recalling War" begins with wounds, surgery, vestigial pain, the legacy of World War I—all seen from the perspective of a backward glance whose distancing is belied by restrained anger posing as a series of paeans to the healing art. The war that maimed and blinded the veterans

> was fought these twenty years ago
> And now assumes the nature-look of time,
> As when the morning traveller turns and views
> His wild night-stumbling carved into a hill.

"What, then, was war?" the second stanza asks. The poem was written in 1938, when it was reasonably clear that the 1914–1918 conflict was about to lose all claim to being the war to end war. The mimicry of philosophic detachment and the ironic use of the past tense (as if war were a quaint anachronism safely relegated to the museum of the past) trigger recollections of the actual sickness of twenty years before:

> What, then, was war? No mere discord of flags
> But an infection of the common sky
> That sagged ominously upon the earth
> Even when the season was the airiest May.

Though "oppressed" by the stupidities of nationalism, the soldiers are described as responding to the pseudo romanticism of war in imagery of adolescent male sexuality. They had "thrust out / Boastful tongue, clenched fist and valiant yard" (here, as in "Ogres and Pygmies," an appropriately obsolescent word for penis), "dying" in a "premature fate-spasm." (We should recall the Beast's phallic emergence from his premature grave in "Saint"—"thrusting out / Wormy from rump to snout.") The sarcasm is the more effective in that it is not directed at the usual straw men of the soldier-poets: the staff officers and the whole "demonic machine, officially sanctioned by a corps of regular padres" (*OP*, p. 539), the detestable fusion of religion and patriotism satirized in that brilliant interaction of war experience and historical scholarship, "The Cuirassiers of the Frontier."[25] The chief enemy in "Recalling War" is that naive romanticism that transformed "fear" into sick, outmoded gestures of gallantry in the face of death: "Never was such antiqueness of romance, / Such tasty honey oozing from the heart."

The last line of the next stanza, with its "ache of wounds beyond all surgeoning," sums up the central theme of the poem thus far, a poem that might have been written by Wilfred Owen. The final stanzas complicate that theme and move the poem closer to Yeats:

> War was return of earth to ugly earth,
> War was foundering of sublimities,
> Extinction of each happy art and faith
> By which the world had still kept head in air,
> Protesting logic or protesting love,
> Until the unendurable moment struck—
> The inward scream, the duty to run mad.

This, the penultimate stanza and the strongest in the poem, recaptures the subtle ambivalence of the opening movement of "Nineteen Hundred and Nineteen." In both poems, genuine anguish for what has been destroyed by war is complicated by insight into the "fine thought," naive optimism, and blind deluded pride which went before a fall that begins to seem, if not just, at least a "return" of a brutal reality that men, babbling of logic or of love, had tried to gloss over or repress. The ultimate theme of both poems is synopsized in Yeats's original manuscript title: "The Things that Come Again."

In the final stanza, Graves employs a familiar comparison:

> And we recall the merry ways of guns—
> Nibbling the walls of factory and church
> Like a child, piecrust; felling groves of trees
> Like a child, dandelions with a switch.
> Machine-guns rattle toy-like from a hill,
> Down in a row the brave tin-soldiers fall.

Referring to international law and supposedly enlightened public opinion as so "many pretty toys," Yeats too depicts a "great army" as but a "showy thing" for parades— "Until," as Graves puts it, "the unendurable moment struck— / The inward scream, the duty to run mad." Then, as

Yeats says, "we" dreamers found ourselves reduced to "weasels fighting in a hole."

> We, who seven years ago
> Talked of honour and of truth,
> Shriek with pleasure if we show
> The weasel's twist, the weasel's tooth.

Graves's language, fusing anger and psychological acuteness, presents an almost Elizabethan world picture, with external historical events reflected in the macrocosm and rooted in the microcosm. "War" was no mere "discord of flags," but a universal "infection of the common sky" and an "inward" scream manifested externally as "the duty to run mad." The result is a pervasive sickness, reminiscent of the *Hamlet*-world, which no prewar "sublimities," no "happy art and faith," were able to paper over—or survive. In the bestial underworld of the trenches, the epitome of a sick culture, the unendurable moment struck—and was, though at enormous cost, endured. The insane vision of a world of malevolent children at their murderous play is indeed, as the final lines of "Recalling War" have it, "A sight to be recalled in elder days / When learnedly the future we devote / To yet more boastful visions of despair."

Like Blake's "marriage hearse" blighted with plagues at the end of "London," Graves's last phrase sardonically telescopes hope and despair. This ancestral prophecy of war is less reckless than Yeats's similar prophecies, including that of "Lapis Lazuli," published in this same year, 1938. But the angry contempt, in part at least self-directed (both poets pointedly refer to "we"), aimed at civilization's rationalistic self-deception and arrogance ("head in air," "learnedly," "Yet more boastful"), is an attitude shared by Yeats and Graves, both of whom insist that the dragons and rough beasts of the underworld must be acknowledged before they can be, if not fully subdued, at least incorporated in a civility that takes account of wildness.

III

The relationship between Graves and Yeats seems to me *the* "interaction" of greatest moment. Its background requires a few words of biography.

"Recalling War" was written in 1938, the last year of the Laura Riding period. Riding and Graves had met in 1926; three years later they left together for Majorca, Graves having just published the classic that was to make him famous (*Good-bye to All That*), but with Riding very much the dominant partner. The poems Graves wrote during this crucial period were more satirical, more vigorously cerebral, and, gradually, richer than anything he had written earlier. The poems of 1929 and after, though still tough-minded and laced with irony, were, many of them, also acute explorations of love and truth as the noblest values in the life both of the individual and of civilization. If the poetry written in the wake of World War I under the influence of the psychiatrist W. H. R. Rivers had been an expression, and sharing, of neurosis, that written under the influence of Laura Riding sought a reality external to the haunted self—a truth attainable only through poetry. "A poem," as the arrogant but incorruptible Riding declared in the preface to her *Collected Poems* (1938), "is an uncovering of truth of so fundamental and general a kind that no other word besides poetry is adequate except truth" (p. xviii). The subjects of this and the next section—Graves's relationship to Yeats and Graves's double-mindedness as poet and mythographer—may be said to pivot on his and Laura Riding's (at one time, for she has since renounced her position) conceptions of truth and poetic integrity.

*   *   *   *

Graves's assault on Yeatsian insincerity began even before his collaboration with Laura Riding. In "The Marmosite's Miscellany" (1925), Graves had employed a garrulous monkey as his mouthpiece for an attack on (among other things) the posturings of Yeats and Eliot. The following year, in their *Survey of Modernist Poetry*, Graves and Riding dismissed Yeats as the exemplar of those poets who "have had neither the courage nor the capacity to go the whole way with modernism and yet have not wished to be left behind." Writing in 1926, they referred with contempt to "Mr. Yeats who, observing that his old poetical robes have worn rather shabby, acquires a new outfit. But the old romantic weaknesses are not so easily discarded: even when he writes of 'Lois Fuller's Chinese Dancers'—a high-brow Vaudeville turn—instead of Eire and the ancient ways, and the Red Rose upon the Rood of Time."[26]

The recent Yeats poem cited—"Nineteen Hundred and Nineteen"—is among the handful of his indisputable masterpieces and, despite the obtuseness of the response here, a poem from which (as we've just seen) Graves has learned. It is hard not to suspect a connection between Graves's attitude toward Yeats and Milton's attitude (as described by Graves) toward John Skelton, "the English poet for whom he felt the strongest antipathy." Graves suspected "restrospective jealousy in Milton, masked as virtuous scorn," for a man praised by the great (Erasmus and Henry VIII, in Skelton's case) and officially "crowned with laurel" (Skelton's laureateship; in Yeats's case, the 1923 Nobel Prize).[27]

Support for the suspicion may be found in Graves's and Riding's vigorous *Pamphlet Against Anthologies* (1928). There the collaborators present an amusing conversation between various anthology favorites. The colloquy ends with "The Lake Isle of Innisfree," which boasts: "My bloke's still alive and he's got the Nobel Prize for being the best poet IN THE WORLD." In the critique of the poem itself, Yeats is pilloried for placing his bean rows, of which there are a pseudo-mystic "nine," too close to the house and for having his linnets, daytime birds, inaccurately filling the "evening" skies. The whole is capped by an epigram entitled "Inisfree on its Author":

> In the Senate house in Dublin
>> My old honest author sits
> Drinking champagne on the proceeds
>> Of his early loss of wits.[28]

If the wit here is genuine, so is the malice—and so is the resentment of Yeats's triumphal progress through the twenties. Juggernauts are rarely appreciated by those under the scythed wheels. While Yeats was a Nobel laureate and no longer an unacknowledged legislator, Graves in 1928 (it would be another year before the publication of *Good-bye to All That*) was a neglected poet whose reputation rested largely on the popular anthology piece "In the Wilderness" (the only poem Graves has retained, incidentally, from his first volume, *Over the Brazier*, 1916). That one poem had earned "six or seven times as much as the total proceeds of the three editions of the volume in which it first appeared" (*Pamphlet*, pp. 92–93). And there, enthroned in the Irish Senate, drinking champagne on *his* proceeds, was that "honest author," Yeats.

When it comes to Yeats, Graves's forehead—like that of "a jealous man" in his excellent poem of that title— "Sweats a fine musk." That the poets have so much in common makes it less remarkable than inevitable that Graves should insist there is nothing between them but distance—and honesty. Yeats, for example, was not a true singer of Eire and the ancient ways. Though "attracted at the age of sixteen by the soft music of Yeats's *Countess Cathleen* and *Wanderings of Oisin*," Graves, whose poems "remain *true* to the Anglo-Irish tradition into which I was born," soon went "behind" Yeats to "literal translations of the Irish texts from which he quarried."[29] Thus the anxious latecomer manages to claim priority—going back, if not to the purity of primary sources, at least to "literal" translations, before they were excavated by Yeats, who, of course, disfigured them by making them over in his own image.

Anglo-Irish romantics whose poetry was tempered and toughened, given intellectual resilience, by their later studies of such poets as Ben Jonson and Donne, Yeats and Graves are also mythographers whose cyclical systems, presided over by lunar Muses, provide metaphors for poetry. The poetry is very often love poetry; and no one, now that its remaining years are countable on fingers and toes, is likely to displace Yeats and Graves as the twentieth century's two preeminent love poets in English. But Graves persists in seeing Yeats through a glass, darkly; and his denunciations of that dishonest author have never abated.

The full-scale attack came in "These Be Your Gods, O Israel!," a refreshing but eccentric assault on the major modernist poets.[30] Though part of a larger offensive, the bludgeoning of Yeats can be extracted and synopsized. Having ticked off the "five living idols" (Yeats, Pound, Eliot, Auden, and Dylan Thomas) who have been set up as objects of "official" veneration, Graves—more bombard captain than critic—attacks in what he acknowledges at the outset to be a lost cause:

> The idols are well-swaddled against anything less destructive than a cobalt bomb; and all my iconoclastic zeal, so far from turning the whole temple blue, will not so much as dent a protective sandbag. Nevertheless, here it comes.
> First, William Butler Yeats.

He began, we are told, reasonably well. Though greedy and lacking a sense of either proportion or humor, the younger Yeats had "wit, industry, a flexible mind, a good ear, and the gift of falling romantically in love—admirable qualities for a beginner." The earliest poems fall short of the pathetic by virtue of their genuine feeling for Ireland and their "irreproachable anvilcraft." But worse times succeeded the former. Graves proceeds to trace the corruption of Yeats—both as artist and man.

The crooked path winds through some chatty, and catty, ad hominem asides. Yeats wrote literary ballads for the "Irish War of Liberation," in which, sniffs Captain Graves, its bard "took no active part." And the suggestion is dropped that, shortly thereafter, the same could be said of the shirker's role in the creation of his own poetry. Yeats, by then using his wife as a medium, told an undergraduate (who told Graves) that he'd written no poems recently—"my wife has been feeling poorly and disinclined."[31] He was somewhat more active, Graves allows, during his stay in Majorca in the spring of 1936. Along with his labors on the Upanishads and the *Oxford Book of Modern Verse*, that was, Graves observes, "the period of his Voronoff operation and its tragi-comic sequels, which were café gossip there for months." (The Steinach rejuvenation operation was actually a few years earlier, and fuller details of the episode with Margot Ruddock are now available.)[32]

While in Majorca, Yeats "wrote asking Laura Riding and myself, as co-authors of *A Survey of Modernist Poetry*, for advice" as to which younger English poets should be included "in his new anthology." When their suggestion, James Reeves, failed to impress Yeats, Graves and Riding "declined to contribute ourselves." This episode is worth discussing, since it seems to have been instrumental in permanently alienating Graves. The issue, again, is one of truth and lying in connection with poetry.

*   *   *   *

Robert Graves's name is to be found in a preliminary list Yeats compiled on 9 October 1935, a list of poets to be included in the Oxford anthology. He intended to print four Graves poems—which four we do not know. At about the same time, Yeats wrote to Graves requesting permission to print the poems. The civility of the response, dated 21 October, was negligible.

He was, Graves began archly, "rather surprised" at the request, for reasons stated "clearly enough" in the *Pamphlet Against Anthologies*. Since then, neither he nor Riding had had a request from any anthologist that "did not recognize our objections and ask whether a special exception might not be made." This was not the case with the present request; indeed, from the poems Yeats asked to use, it seemed to Graves that what was being created was "an enlarged Yeats anthology—a sort of Yeatsian . . . Spectre." Whatever the legitimate concern of poets that anthologists might distort or misrepresent their work, the final two paragraphs of Graves's letter are as haughty as Yeats at his worst; there is even, apparently, an ungracious refusal of Yeats's request to visit the collaborators the following spring, when he would be in Majorca. "I do not know whether a letter from you to Laura Riding is on the way from some forwarding address," Graves wrote:

> But if so, the answer for both of us, your anthology being what it seems to be (from the indication of those four poems of mine and from the absence of any awareness in you that we do not lend ourselves to any but cooperative activities), would have to be, I think, No.
>
> We are both very watchful in our relations, whether in literature or in neighbour-ship: never casual, and least of all here in Majorca where we live permanently in hard-working privacy. With the many foreigners who visit the island we have, as a rule, nothing to do—unless they are friends of ours, who come here purposely to see us. Certainly we like to get to know new people and especially those with whom there may be something in common; but we are not sure what there might be in common between you and L.R. (someone in a press-cutting a few months ago said that you and she had both learned things from each other—but certainly L.R. does not go about "learning" from people) and between you and me; and we hate mere literary-name fraternizing—but perhaps you feel the same about that.
>
> Yours sincerely,
> Robert Graves[33]

Graves and Riding were obviously miffed that Yeats had not written to her as well—both as a poet and as a partner in their exclusively "cooperative activities." There was no request "on the way" to her. In a letter written in April of the following year, Yeats told Dorothy Wellesley that he'd reconsidered (at Dorothy's suggestion) Laura Riding, whom he'd originally rejected. Newly impressed, he had written to her requesting three poems: "Lucrece and Nara," "The Wind Suffers," and "The Flowering Urn." He added that she would probably refuse, "as Graves has."[34]

Though Graves claims that *both* declined to contribute,

though apparently more for their own reasons than because of the Reeves rejection, Laura didn't *quite* refuse; and the issue *was* wider. As Yeats said, she insisted on conditions he felt unable to accept: "must see introduction, must see list of contents, must not take anything already in any other anthology." Yeats replied "politely," pointing out, however, that he was a "despotic man" and offering "nothing." Riding's response was no less unequivocal:

> I for one lend myself to no despotic objects, domestic or public. . . . I recognize no personal table of values, least of all in poetry. Poems vary, but the values of poetry are not variable; and in my opinion any special view imposed upon poetry is destructive. This is why I regard anthologies as destructive.[35]

Graves's refusal was evidently unconditional. And the dismissal of Reeves (a friend of Graves's to this day), particularly Yeats's explanation of the dismissal, cut to the rankling heart of the matter. The rejection, Graves recalled in his Clark lecture twenty years later, was accompanied by "this really devilish comment: 'Too reasonable, too truthful. We poets should be good liars, remembering always that the Muses are women and prefer the embrace of gay, warty lads.' " Graves and his Muse were not amused. The doctrine of Nietzsche's Zarathustra, particularly as funneled through Yeats's randy mask of Wild Old Wicked Man, was repellent to both collaborators: to Graves, who was, Riding told a mistaken Yeats, "in *no* sense of the word," physical or mystical, her "husband," and to Riding herself, who had made Graves her coapostle of integrity and truthfulness in poetry.

And the allusion to Zarathustra's "We poets lie too much" would have been missed by neither. One of the volumes Riding recommended to Yeats was her collection *Poet: A Lying Word* (1933); and Graves, in the essay he wrote on Nietzsche at just this time, quotes the *Dionysus-Dithyrambs* of Nietzsche, which Zarathustra is echoing: "Only the poet who can lie / Wilfully, skilfully / Can tell the truth." The doctrine is mocked by Graves in a sardonic advice-poem of the thirties: "To forge a picture that will pass for true, / Do conscientiously what liars do," a variation on the more celebrated satire aimed at the people who gave Zarathustra his name, "The Persian Version." Doubtless, the first poem, "The Devil's Advice to Story-Tellers," was in Graves's mind when he referred to Yeats's Zarathustrian comment as "really devilish."[36]

That Yeats's cavalierly Nietzschean attitude toward truth was intolerable to Graves is confirmed earlier in the Clark lecture. There Graves had vilified Yeats's observation, made in a letter to Sturge Moore, that he "preferred the violent expression of error (as in Bernard Shaw or Schopenhauer) to the reasonable expression of truth which corrupts by its lack of pugnacity." Here, Graves, who despite his indebtedness to Nietzsche dismissed him as a "mad German ox," probably missed the allusion; writing of Schopenhauer, Nietzsche said, "The errors of great men are venerable because they are more fruitful than the truths of little men."[37] But of course he did not miss the application of the doctrine to Reeves, whose verse Yeats grandly pronounced "Too truthful, too reasonable." The slight to Reeves and to his cosponsors was subsumed under a larger heading, impudence modulating into "devilish" blasphemy against the Muse, who demands truthfulness no less than subservience in her acolytes. Here was proof that Yeats was (as Graves and Riding declared in a 1937 essay reacting in part to this correspondence) a writer who believed "in poems but not in poetry"; proof that he was one of those worshiped idols whose rites were, as Graves put it in the Clark lecture, "quite incompatible with devotion to the Muse herself."[38]

Yeats was, in his own work, "Irishman enough," Graves granted, to realize the need to augment craftsmanship with "grace," defined as "the presence of the Muse Goddess." But she does not appear, Graves warns, "unless her poet has something urgent to say and to win her consent a poet *must* have something urgent to say." There was indeed a new Yeats: "new, well-groomed, cynical," a "buccaneer and smart-stepping salesman" whose "transmogrification" was "largely the work of Ezra Pound," a "mad dog" for whom Graves has never had anything but contempt. This later

Yeats "had a new technique, but nothing to say. . . . Instead of the Muse, he employed a ventriloquist's dummy called Crazy Jane. But still he had nothing to say."

It may be, as Graves declares elsewhere (*OP*, p. 245), that "No man can decently speak in a woman's name"; and of course the great sin against the spirit, "according to Graves's and Riding's moral principles," is "assuming a personality not your own." I am quoting from Michael Kirkham's discussion of "To Evoke Posterity," Graves's fine satire on the would-be "great" poet who has a palpable design on the reader whose approval he seeks as the guarantor of his immortality. What Kirkham (p. 150) calls Graves's "finely concentrated phrase" for this process of assuming another personality in order to evoke posterity—"Ventriloquizing for the unborn"—is likely to have been in Graves's mind when he described Yeats's Crazy Jane as a "ventriloquist's dummy."

Graves cites "To Evoke Posterity"—significantly, to illustrate the violation of "poetic integrity"—in the Clark lecture immediately preceding the attack on Yeats (*OP*, p. 118). And if the poem's opening reference to ventriloquism looks forward to the remark on Yeats, its final stanza looks *back* on Yeats—to the 1910 poem "Against Unworthy Praise," in which "proud" abhorrence of "dolt and knave" is mingled with an acknowledged need for public applause: "What, still you would have their praise!" In Graves's version, the honored man is already dead, but recognizably Yeatsian, masked and cast in bronze:

> Alive, you have abhorred
> The crowds on holiday
> Jostling and whistling—yet would you air
> Your death-mask, smoothly lidded,
> Along the promenade?

Kirkham's thematic synopsis is immediately germane to Graves's (and Riding's) response to Yeats, in the twenties and later: "The poem finds in this betrayal of self the single, unifying explanation of all the falsities of public life. Pursuing not the truth of self but public applause, you will lose personal reality and *become* the empty thing owned by the public." And for that, says the poem,

> the punishment is fixed:
> To be found fully ancestral,
> To be cast in bronze for a city square,
> To dribble green in times of rain
> And stain the pedestal.

The punishment, in short, is to be one of the official but hollow idols attacked or, rather, defecated on in "These Be Your Gods, O Israel!"

Graves concludes the critical generalities of his iconoclastic lecture by agreeing with Raymond Mortimer's accurate description of Yeats as "a bower bird collecting bright coloured rags and pebbles from the Hebrew *Kabbalah*, the *Vedanta*, the *Mabinogion*, the alchemists, Swedenborg, Blake, Nietzsche, and the Theosophists," but not with Mortimer's contention that Yeats hammered these eclectic materials "into hard and burnished gold" in poetry of "terseness, tensity, and eloquence." The arcana remain for Graves so much hard, burnished "rubbish."[39] As for the rubbish of what Yeats has Crazy Jane call "Heart's truth"— elsewhere, that "mound of refuse" and "foul rag-and-bone shop of the heart" in which Yeats says he must at least "lie down"—Graves believes only the "lie," a devilish one. In his own poem "Hell," written a decade before Yeats's "The Circus Animals' Desertion," Graves describes a great sack out of which a gleeful devil feeds damned souls. It contains "Husks, rags and bones, waste-paper, excrement"; but it is all lifeless fare, the refuse not of heart's truth but of dishonest verbiage, with which the devil feeds "his false five thousands."

Graves's contemptuous dismissals of Yeats's ventriloquism and Yeats's poetic utilization of esoteric "rubbish" fuse in his commentary on "Chosen." This is the poem he seizes on as a representative production of the "new-model Yeats": a Yeats "em-Pounded," in Graves's backhanded compliment, "as far as he was capable." The lecturer confines himself to the second of the poem's two stanzas:

> I struggled with the horror of daybreak,
> I chose it for my lot! If questioned on
> My utmost pleasure with a man
> By some new-married bride, I take
> That stillness for a theme
> Where his heart my heart did seem
> And both adrift on the miraculous stream
> Where—wrote a learned astrologer—
> The Zodiac is changed into a sphere.

The opening artillery barrage is trained on Yeats's use of half-rhymes, a point to which we'll return. Next to be deplored is the stanza's "imprecision," which Graves finds compounded rather than clarified by the note supplied in the 1933 edition of *The Winding Stair and Other Poems*:

> The "learned astrologer" in *Chosen* was Macrobius, and the particular passage was found for me by Dr. Sturm, that too little known poet and mystic. It is from Macrobius's comment upon "Scipio's Dream" (Lib. I, Cap. XII, Sec. 5): ". . . when the sun is in Aquarius, we sacrifice to the Shades, for it is in the sign inimical to human life; and from thence, the meeting-place of Zodiac and Milky Way, the descending soul by its defluction is drawn out of the spherical, the sole divine form, into the cone."

In the poem, Yeats has varied—indeed, reversed—his Neoplatonic source. For it is true, as Graves notes, that Macrobius did not say that the zodiac becomes a sphere, but rather that the *soul*, having reached a certain point in the zodiac, is drawn *from* the sperical form *into* the conical. (Graves's objection had, incidentally, been anticipated by Frank Pearce Sturm, though Sturm was objecting to the original, and inaccurate, version of the note, not to Yeats's poetic license.) Graves feigns bewilderment even about the corrected note: "But what that means, even Dr. Sturm has not elucidated."

As Graves has said (in the foreword to the 1938 *Collected Poems*), "Poems do or do not stand by their poetic meaning: learned explanations [by their authors] cannot give them more than they possess" (p. xiv). Surely, however, most readers, few if any of us as erudite as the author of *The White Goddess*, perceive the sexual analogue of this transformation of the restless cone (the whirling zodiacal gyre of the poem's opening stanza) into the motionless sphere—symbol of perfection not only for the Latin encyclopedist Macrobius but for rather less obscure thinkers, Parmenides and Plato among them. Quite aside from the irony that the charge is being made by the man who wrote such poems as "To Juan at the Winter Solstice" and "The Ambrosia of Dionysus and Semele," Graves's parting slap—that it is an act of "impudence" to "Dame Ocupacyon" to publish a poem "strewn with references to which not one reader in ten million has the key"[40]—loses much of its sting when the offending lines are examined in context: the context both of this poem as a whole and of the sequence of which it is the nucleus and pivot.

Graves has taken neither context into account. If he had, he could hardly have committed the astonishing gaffe of taking the speaker of this poem to be "some man," even Yeats himself.[41] "Chosen" is the sixth and central lyric of the concentrically structured sequence *A Woman Young and Old*. In all but the framing poems, I and XI, the speaker is the titular woman. Yet Graves, taking the lines

> If questioned on
> My utmost pleasure with a man
> By some new-married bride

charges Yeats with syntactical awkwardness and confusion: the bride's question "seems to pre-suppose sexual commerce between Yeats and a man, not her husband." Maybe no man *can* "decently speak in a woman's name," but this grotesque misreading violates more than matters of persona and context. It is tone-deaf, oblivious not only to the woman's moment of ecstasy recollected in tranquillity, but also to her qualifying urbanity. Graves attacks the "imprecision" of "the astrologer's remark that 'The Zodiac is changed into a sphere' " and the explanatory note appended by the poet. This seems legitimate criticism; but then he fails to examine the very stanza he quotes: the lines that give the astrological allusion (in R. P. Blackmur's phrase) its "only excuse for *poetic* being."

Not that Yeats's imagery and "learned explanation" are

frivolous; the zodiacal iconography, present in the sequence as early as poem III, is an important part of the symbolic structure of the eleven-poem set. At the same time, one detects a note of sophisticated, tongue-in-cheek humor in the woman's comparison of the moment of postcoital stillness to the drifting of hearts on the miraculous stream, "Where— wrote a learned astrologer— / The Zodiac is changed into a sphere." When, at the very height of her description of sexual ecstasy, she cites an abstruse text, the woman mimics the simultaneous detachment and participation of the scholarly man of letters. In a rather Irish comic spirit, she seems a half-serious parody of the poet who created her, partially detached from the reality that she describes, at the same time both in and out of ecstasy, a scholar of the scene as well as a participant.[42]

The woman takes her Neoplatonic astrology with some seriousness. But from what we know of her temperament (in the preceding poem she had stood Neoplatonic doctrine on its head with a *felix-culpa* variation emphasizing the intensification of sexual pleasure), she would not be solemnly pedantic in the present imagined setting, questioned by a new-married bride on her "utmost pleasure with a man." To have her answer as she does with *no* saving urbanity would be to parody the role assigned by Dryden to Donne, who "perplexes the minds of the fair sex with nice speculations of philosophy, when he should engage their hearts and entertain them with the softness of love." I am assuming that the new-married bride has not come fresh from a perusal of *A Vision*, or of Donne (the stanza, meter, and imagery of whose "Nocturnall upon S. Lucies Day" Yeats borrows for "Chosen"), or of Macrobius, and also that she has not been corresponding with "that too little known mystic and poet, Dr. Sturm."

Aside from tone, there is a skeptical caveat present in the word *seem*: "Where his heart my heart did *seem*." That embedded disclaimer of the whole assertion has been carefully calculated, not slipped in merely to make a rhyme. In one of the late drafts of the poem, Yeats had "My heart *became* his heart." He could easily have placed "became" at the end of the line (he was to end up with an inversion in any case). Yeats would certainly not have been disturbed by an oblique rhyme, a favorite device employed (to Graves's annoyance) in the immediately preceding lines: "on / . . . man." In another draft, *seemed* is included in the formulation, though *not* required by the rhyme scheme. What troubled Yeats and caused him to cancel *became* was his unwillingness to make, or have the woman make, so absolute an assertion.

Ironically, Graves had touched on the question of "doubt" in discussing Yeats's improper use of oblique rhyming. Yeats's "bold poetic licences" included rhyming "astronomer" with "sphere" and "on" with "man." Such half-rhymes, says Graves, are "justified by poetic necessity only where a prevailing mood of gloom, doubt, mental stress or confusion would be denied by too perfect an answering rhyme." Precisely; and a careful reading of "Chosen" would have revealed it to be a poem in which the speaker, a woman recalling her struggle with the horror of daybreak and separation from her lover, celebrates the precarious (perhaps illusory) moment of love and concludes by describing it in a tone that, compounded of ecstasy and urbane mock-pedantry, conveys sophisticated doubt as well as mystical transport. The theme and tonal ambivalence are sufficiently similar to those found in some Graves poems, the double-mindedness so "Gravesian," that one might have expected a sensitive reading. It is enough to raise the question whether, here and elsewhere, Graves is not engaged in what Harold Bloom calls creative misreading: the *clinamen* or anxious swerve away from a precursor by whom one feels overshadowed or even preempted.

*　　*　　*　　*

Yvor Winters was notoriously of the opinion that Sturge Moore was a better poet than his friend Yeats, a notion that has never really caught on. In the peroration of his lecture, Graves drops a similarly bizarre bombshell: "William Davies, though at times his simplicity degenerated into artfulness, put his near contemporary Yeats to shame" (*OP*, p. 151). In an earlier lecture in the series, Graves had quoted a poem by W. H. Davies, one he admired for its "passionate detachment" and "troubled ambiguity" (*OP*, p. 119). Both of these are qualities, one would have thought, of the man who wanted to write poems "as cold and passionate as the dawn" and who *had* written "Easter 1916." But then Yeats had taken "no active part" in the Easter Rising and had sacrificed integrity to a passionate intensity attracted to the violent expression of error, not to the reasonable expression of truth. Like the Persians praised by Herodotus, cited though not emulated by Nietzsche's Zarathustra, and accused of mendacity by Graves ("The Persian Version"), the true Muse poet must, it seems, bear arms skillfully as well as tell the truth. Graves notes that Yeats and Eliot did not bear arms in Ireland or in France; and Auden, who "went to Spain in warlike ardour by a comrade's side . . . saw no fighting," though he did get in "plenty of ping-pong in a hotel at Sitges." The physical courage and integrity all these "idols" lacked was possessed by Alun Lewis, a poet killed in World War II. Graves concludes "These Be Your Gods, O Israel!" by citing a letter written by Lewis "from the Welch regiment in Burma to his Muse in Wales":

> My longing is more and more for one thing only, integrity, and I discount the other qualities in people ruthlessly if they lack that fundamental sincerity and wholeness.[43]

It is under the twin banners of the old regiment and of the integrity and truthfulness due the Muse that Captain Graves of the Welch Fusiliers bombards the entrenched idols, these false gods and graven images of modernist criticism. Only two of the five idols are granted what Lewis calls "other qualities"; but Eliot died early as a poet, and the later Yeats, seduced into literary modernism, "aimed deliberately off-target" (*OP*, p. 149). Both, especially Yeats, had therefore to be savaged, in Lewis's word, "ruthlessly." In the last of his Oxford lectures, eleven years later, Graves returned to the case of the artist who, succumbing to the current fashion, tries to "*out-zeitgeist* the *zeitgeist*." The "saddest" cases, we are told,

> are artists who begin with a small genuine individual craft, but, enraged by imitators, decide to start a new, theatrical gimmicky style, instead of perfecting the genuine one by an inclusion of all deeper or darker sides of their nature, hitherto concealed, to the point at which it can no longer be imitated.

Here again the central target seems to be Yeats. In the Clark lecture, Graves—getting his allusions right but his chronology fouled—had traced the emergence in the twenties of a new Yeats, tough and with singing-robes cast away, to the complaint that he had been "plagued by a swarm of imitators."[44] Lest there be any doubt that it is the shadow of the later Yeats that still darkens Graves's imagination in the Oxford lecture, he becomes immediately, and ruthlessly, specific:

> The same phenomenon appears among poets. W. B. Yeats, a careful craftsman, who began with strong literary principles, was later seduced into a period of grandiose literary showmanship. I find the later, strutting Senator Yeats a pathetic, rather than a commanding, figure. (*OP*, pp. 581–82)

Graves is neither the first nor the last to have been put off by the strutting of later Yeats. But the failure to penetrate the surface of the theatrical posture ("There struts Hamlet, there is Lear") or of the deliberately adopted mask (supplied first by Wilde, hardened and burnished with the help of Nietzsche and Swift), or to separate the man from the work, seems total—and, without the context of "interaction" I have tried to supply here, more than a little bewildering.

The passage of the decade between the two series of lectures had only exacerbated Graves's detestation. To the point, apparently, where he was blind to the fact that his own recommendation—that the poet ought to perfect his "genuine" gift by including all the deeper or darker sides of his own inimitable nature—was precisely the program Yeats had followed in transforming himself from a denizen of the Celtic Twilight into the poet of *The Tower*, *The Winding Stair*, and such last poems as "Lapis Lazuli," "The Circus Animals'

Desertion," "The Man and the Echo," and, above all, "Cuchulain Comforted." From the last two poems in particular, both death poems, Yeats emerges, stripped of his Nietzschean gestures, as precisely what Graves and Riding had mocked ten years earlier: an "old honest author." Even Graves should have been able to see, and to acknowledge, Yeats's exploration of the dark depths of his own ambivalent nature, especially his adoption of the mask of a woman, dismissed by Graves as phony, posterity-evoking ventriloquism. And even *Captain* Graves might have seen some point at least in the question Yeats asked and answered in notes prepared for a lecture of his own: "Why should we honor those that die on the field of battle. A man may show as reckless a courage in entering into the abyss of himself."[45]

IV

But Robert Graves, for whom battlefields are more than metaphors, is hardly a man who needs to be lectured to on the subjects of courage and integrity. During the Great War, Graves had found himself

> among men whom detestable trench conditions and persistent danger either destroyed or ennobled. . . . Holding a trench to the last round of ammunition and the last man, taking a one-in-three chance of life when rescuing a badly wounded comrade from no-man's-land, keeping up a defiant pride in our soldierly appearance: these were poetic virtues. Our reward lay in their practice, with possible survival as a small bright light seen at the end of a long tunnel.

After the war, Graves "swore a poetic oath never again to be anyone's servant but my own," and the defiant pride that characterized the fusilier henceforth governed the poet's service to his craft and his Muse (*OP*, p. 539).

The soldierly virtues of courage, skill, and endurance served Graves well during the triumph of modernism. While Eliot, Pound, and the later ("em-Pounded") Yeats were monopolizing the attention, Graves went on practicing his art. "He wasn't sulking in his tent," said one critic who shares Graves's disdain of the gods installed in the modernist pantheon; "he had gone on writing and publishing."[46] His reward would seem to have come in the form of the Muse's sudden revelation of her mysteries to her dedicated vassal. The craftsman was to become the champion of the Goddess: "Unworthy as I am, I am her man."[47]

As with so many modern poets, the most characteristic work of Graves, whose "last Christian-minded poem" ("In the Wilderness") is the very first in all the collections, takes as one of its beginnings the pronouncement of the death of the Judeo-Christian God. Graves's tone—far from the ostensibly joyful but actually heartbroken cry of Nietzsche—has the cheerfulness of Wallace Stevens. For Stevens, the poet replaces empty heaven and its hymns; for Graves,

A dying superstition smiles and hums
"Abide with me"—God's evening hymn, not ours.

But the poet, in Graves's version, does not enter the vacuum left by God; in his matriarchal religion "Cerridwen abides," and the "simple loving declaration . . . made implicitly or explicitly by all true Muse-poets since poetry began" is " 'None greater in the universe than the Triple Goddess!' " (*WG*, pp. 448, 492). But is it all, as in Stevens's case, the weaving of a Supreme Fiction?

If so, Graves is among the *philalethes*, friends of truth, and, simultaneously, the fabricator of the longest-running Supreme Fiction in twentieth-century literature. The will to truth and the telling of his "one story" may not seem contradictory to Graves, who might simply respond that the White Goddess "story" happens to be "true." But what for him is religion is for the rest of us mythology, and Graves himself, on at least one significant occasion, was disarmingly skeptical. We seem to have another instance of Graves's wild civility: here, the interaction of speculative foolhardiness and sadomasochism with sophisticated intellectuality and a balancing emphasis on truth. It is in connection with the

Goddess, celebrated both as the source of truth and for her power and capacity for vengeance, that the chief tension seems to reside. We might·begin to trace this interaction, which will once again involve us in comparison with Yeats, by turning to Graves's most spellbound and visceral evocation of the primordial blood rites associated with the White Goddess.

"The main theme of poetry is, properly, the relations of man and woman," writes Graves. The true poet is granted a temporary paradise, but he is doomed, "and the poet knows that it must be so." For him there is no other woman but Cerridwen, the Welsh White Goddess of Life-in-Death and Death-in-Life. She will "gladly give him her love, but at only one price: his life." With her love "goes wisdom," but she will exact payment "punctually and bloodily."

> Cerridwen abides. Poetry began in the matriarchal age, and derives its magic from the moon, not from the sun. No poet can hope to understand the nature of poetry unless he has had a vision of the Naked King crucified to the lopped oak, and watched the dancers, red-eyed from the acrid smoke of the sacrificial fires, stamping out the measure of the dance, their bodies bent uncouthly forward, with a monotonous chant of: "Kill! kill! kill!" and "Blood! blood! blood!" (WG, pp. 447–48)

We have arrived at the heart of darkness, with Graves, less a Marlow than a Kurtz at this point, joining the ritualists for a dance and a howl. Darkly exciting as it is, a little of this goes a long way. But if we are tempted to repeat what has been said of Yeats's mythopoeia in *A Vision*—that a little seems too much, his business none of ours—we ought to remember, too, that such business, however extravagant, *may* be ours, especially if we hope to understand the nature of poetry. To think otherwise would be to forget what we have learned, not only or even essentially from Graves, but also from Conrad and Mann, Yeats and Lawrence, and, of course, from Nietzsche and Frazer before them. It is not Nietzsche—some of whose perorations sound as sadomasochistic as this one by Graves—but that academic recorder of the persistence of the primitive, Sir James Frazer, who reminds us that while the "mystic doctrines and extravagant rites" of Dionysus worship "were essentially foreign to the clear intelligence and sober temperament of the Greek race," that religion nevertheless spread like wildfire through Greece, "appealing as it did to that love of mystery and that proneness to revert to savagery which seems to be innate in most men."

Like most men (Frazer included), Graves shares this Attic dualism. However "foreign" to his clear intelligence and sober temperament, the mysterious and savage religion of the Goddess certainly appeals to him. Discussing Graves as mythographer, Patrick Grant has rightly observed that only a formidable intellect could conceive of so complex and syncretic a figure as the White Goddess; that while his mythography depends on what Graves calls the "logic of myth" (*WG*, p. 321), his Historical Grammar is "evidently the product of an enormously sophisticated post-Cartesian mind." Graves's own attitude suggests "a further ambivalence," Grant continues;

> for it is sometimes hard to reconcile the vast subtlety with which the figure of the White Goddess is presented with what seem to be frequent yearnings on Graves's part for simple primitivism, and as "the ancient power of fright and lust" [*WG*, p. 24] . . . she exerts more power on Graves' imagination than in her aspect of lover. Graves is fascinated by the cruel rites which accompany her worship, or characterize her nature.

Commenting on the combination of bestial violence, blatant sexuality, and treachery "not uncharacteristic of Graves' ruminations on the Goddess," Grant finds "an uneasy relationship" between his fascination for this side of the Goddess and his fascination for the other, in which she appears in a host of disguises and paradigms of "complexly interrelated cultural significance."[48]

Granted his attraction to primitivism, Graves remains a post-Renaissance man, highly self-conscious and fully aware of what he is after. What he is after, he says, is truth. It is characteristic that he should immediately follow the chant of "Kill! kill! kill! . . . Blood! blood! blood!" with this sentence: "Constant illiterate use of the phrase 'to woo the Muse' has obscured its poetic sense: the poet's inner communion with the White Goddess, regarded as the source of truth" (*WG*, p. 448). Such a statement returns us to the question of the relationship between truth and the myth; to the problematic status of Graves as both scholar and acolyte of his Muse; and to the ontological status of the Goddess herself.

*   *   *   *

There is in Graves an abiding impulse to reveal the essential. The sacred duty of the "true poet" is to tell the Muse-goddess "the truth about himself and her in his own passionate and peculiar words" (*WG*, p. 444). Even that formulation is equivocal, and Graves's peculiar words—in poems, mythography, and historical fiction—tell us more about him than about the numinous Goddess. But his will to truth, though as problematic as Nietzsche's, remains a unifying principle. From poems as apparently light as "The Persian Version," through the dispersion of "lies" and illusions in such poems as "Recalling War," "End of Play," and "A Love Story," to the higher "magical" truths of "To Juan at the Winter Solstice" and "The White Goddess," the one story worth telling has involved the climactic imperative, which, according to Herodotus, characterized those Persians mocked by Graves for violating it: "To tell the truth." But of course Nietzsche's Persian, Zarathustra, also quoted the encomium of Herodotus—only, as we've seen, to admit that "we poets lie too much."

Nevertheless, Graves insists on the quest for truth. The impulse behind his textual "restorations" and his historical fiction is the same: to recover the "real" facts beneath the received distortions. Graves's position is radically skeptical. Just as establishment poets and critics have engaged in an Apollonian conspiracy to falsify poetic history, so professional historians have conspired with the passage of time to distort the facts, to paint an inch thick the features of Clio. Graves is almost Nietzschean in his contempt for the official *pia fraus*. But in his genealogical passion to disclose "what really happened" he is laying claim to the legacy of another German: his own ancestor, the great historian Leopold von Ranke. "To him I owe my historical method," says Graves. But the historical results are rather different.

This passion to "recover" the truth concealed by biased official versions, not exactly alien to our age of investigative reporting, has stimulated genuine discovery and crackpot revisionism. Between these extremes lies a vast amount of conspiracy-theory detective work; and Graves, both as scholar and historical novelist, has been part of it. In passages of *The White Goddess* (pp. 261, 449) that illuminate the interaction between Graves's splendid poem "Sick Love" and the biblical text that supplies its title, Graves tells us what is "really" happening in the love songs of the Canticles. His novelistic contribution to Samuel Butler's congenial theory that Homer was a woman is *Homer's Daughter* (1955), the last of Graves's novels, in which we learn that the author of the *Odyssey* was a Sicilian princess, the Nausicaa of the poem. From the time of his first novel, revealingly entitled *The Real David Copperfield*, Graves has been hot in pursuit of the real.[49]

Much scholarship in the *historia arcana* tradition has centered on Christ. Graves sees his Christological reconstructions, revealing "the secret history of Jesus" (*King Jesus*, p. 13), as part of the continuing quest for the historical Jesus. *King Jesus* (1946), a novel composed "by the analeptic method," and *Jesus in Rome* (1957), subtitled "A Historical Conjecture," are certainly in this tradition. To fully appreciate Graves's mythographic skill in placing the "true" Christ within the pattern of the White Goddess's ultimate revenge on patriarchy, we might approach *King Jesus* by way of a later work, one not ostensibly fictitious, but certainly analeptic.

In that work, *Hebrew Myths: The Book of Genesis* (1964), Graves, after positing that an ancient matriarchal culture existed in prebiblical times, argues, as he'd had Mary the Hairdresser argue in chapter 19 of *King Jesus*, that a deliberate suppression of Goddess-worship resulted in the "patriarchal and monotheistic" myths of a later period, including the

authoritarian monotheism of the Old Testament. In this con-
jectural reshaping, the prime target of Jehovah's puritanical
vengeance was, of course, the White Goddess. That usurpa-
tion of female power must in time be revenged—as part of
which inexorable cycle the New Testament is made, in
Graves's reconstruction in *King Jesus*, to fulfill the Old in a
way undreamt of by orthodox exegetes.

Graves's Jesus, the son of a temple virgin clandestinely
married to Herod Antipater, is "this last and noblest scion of
the most venerable royal line in the world" (*KJ*, p. 14). But he
also, sharing the Jewish "obsession with celestial patriarchy," is an antimatriarchal fanatic single-mindedly devoted
to the God of Israel. The Gravesian Christ "dies,"[50] not as he
had intended (by the sword of one of his male followers), but
on the cross, attended by the three Marys: the Virgin, Mary
the Hairdresser, and Mary of Cleopas, the sister of Lazarus,
to whom (according to Graves) the celibate Jesus was be-
trothed but from whom he sexually abstained, consistent
with his grand design "to break the lamentable cycle of birth,
procreation, death and rebirth" (*KJ*, p. 284). This female
trinity constitutes the Triple Goddess. Such an identification
had long since been proposed by heretical Copts (*WG*, pp.
142–43). But in the novel—which, reusing the device so bril-
liantly exploited in the Claudius novels, purports to be a
translation of a recovered ancient manuscript—Graves establishes a rich politico-religious context to support his culminat-
ing revaluation of all values: a reversal of the tablets that takes
the form of the flouted Goddess's reassertion of her power.
For in his unintended ritual death by crucifixion, Jesus

> ironically becomes the maimed and hanged god of the waxing
> year, re-absorbed by the matriarchal powers he had de-
> nounced but within which his career was both instituted and
> developed. The three Marys who watch him die represent the
> White Goddess in her three aspects as mother, lover, and
> layer-out.[51]

Here, in *King Jesus*, as almost everywhere else, Graves's
immense erudition, synthesis of detail, and sheer ingenuity
(the book is at least as learned and speculatively fertile as

Morton Smith's 1978 *Jesus the Magician*) are marshaled in the service of a fascinating but polemical and reductive monomyth, a totalitarianism of the ubiquitous Goddess. And, however antithetical she may be to Jehovah, the message is the same: Vengeance is mine. Significantly, this same motif of delayed but inevitable vengeance shapes the climactic chapter of *The White Goddess*. Climactic, that is, in 1948: a "Postscript" was later appended, with what tempering effect we shall see.

The original final chapter, a tract for the times, opens portentously: "What, then, is to be the future of religion in the West?" (*WG*, p. 474). That question and Graves's chiliastic stance ("I foresee no change for the better until everything gets far worse"), taken together with the chapter's still more portentous title, "The Return of the Goddess," all suggest to me a recollection on Graves's part of Yeats's triad of apocalyptic poems: "Nineteen Hundred and Nineteen" (entitled, in draft, "The Things that Come Again"), "The Gyres," and, especially, "The Second Coming." The suspicion is certainly reinforced by the tone and imagery of "The Destroyers," the poem with which Graves ends *The White Goddess*.[52]

Of course, in Graves's uxorious vision, the desired good that shall succeed mere anarchy—what he calls "a period of complete political and religious disorganization" (*WG*, p. 484)—is restored Goddess-worship. But the apocalyptic imagery and the mixture of titillation, terror, and longing for the day to come, all of which we associate preeminently with Yeats, are abundantly present. "The longer her hour is postponed," we are told by her prophet, the "less merciful" will she be. Waiting "in terror of the judgment day," we must placate her by assuming the "worst" (*WG*, p. 486). Graves ends the chapter, and his book, with a poem memorializing "the man who first tilted European civilization off balance, by enthroning the restless and arbitrary male will . . . and dethroning the female sense of orderliness." The poem is a "satire . . . we owe her," and the purpose of satire, according to Graves, is "to destroy whatever is overblown . . . and clear the way for a new sowing" (*WG*, p. 446).

The satirized man turns out to be Perseus, type of the male conqueror. It was that "mailed wonder of mankind"—sword-bearing and "capped with lunar gold / Like an old and savage dunce"—who "dared seize" the throne of the sacrificial consort of the moon. The allusion to Blake's "The Tyger," which Graves thought a poem of "tremendous impact," is unmistakable. In fact, in his second Oxford lecture, Graves "improved" Blake's poem by changing his tense: from "dare seize" to "dared seize," the form in which it appears here. The echo of "The Tyger" moves us closer to "The Second Coming," whose wrathful beast slouches in the apocalyptic shadow of Blake's beast, but which is presumably *not* a poem admired by Graves. In fact, I suspect that the final stanza of Graves's prophecy of the violent return of the Goddess combines Yeats's thrilled anticipation of cataclysmic reversal with an attack on Yeatsian values.

> Gusts of laughter the Moon stir
> That her Bassarids now bed
> With the unnoble usurer,
> While an ignorant pale priest
> Rides the beast with a man's head
> To her long-omitted feast.

In the preceding chapter, Graves had said, "The White Goddess in her orgiastic character seems to have no chance of staging a comeback until women themselves grow weary of decadent patriarchalism, and turn Bassarids again."[53] Here, the Bassarids have been bedded by usurers. Though it was Ezra Pound who most prominently set the ancient fertility cults against the sterile crime of usury, the central allusions are Yeatsian. Whatever its other arcane, historical, and anthropological sources, this "beast with a man's head" recalls Yeats's "rough beast" with "lion body and the head of a man." The ignorant pale priest riding that creature to the long-omitted feast of the moon goddess may echo the "pale-eyed priest" of Milton's nativity ode, deliberately transformed by Keats into a "pale-mouthed prophet" in his own celebration of a long-omitted feast in honor of a female deity, the neglected goddess Psyche. But Graves's pale priest, no prophet dreaming, is an ignorant destroyer. "Ignorant" is a Yeatsian adjective, often honorific (as when he celebrates those "great ignorant leafy ways" of prelapsarian bliss). I suspect that Graves is thinking of Yeats himself as the ignorant shaman riding his own rough beast (one that excites the older poet almost as much as it terrifies him) to a feast other than the one he expects. For the dispensation to come, according to Graves, is not the "harsh, masculine, *antithetical*" civilization Yeats projects in *A Vision* and in his long note to "The Second Coming." The new dispensation will be harsh but *feminine*—a civilization, to quote Graves's "The Second-Fated," "Under the sceptre of Guess Whom?"

Graves's poem, which he specifically designates a "satire," may be directed not only at destroyer Perseus but also at destruction-loving Yeats. If so, what Graves misses, it seems to me, is the deepest tonality of "The Second Coming." For the real surprise of that poem, beyond the *èpater les bourgeois* theme that the *Parousia* will take a very different "shape" than that expected by naive, orthodox Christians, is that Yeats's own dream will be shattered; that the new age will not assume the shape of an aristocratic civilization but, rather, that of the chaos its brutal engendering prefigures. With that deeper insight, both the theoretician and the cold-eyed oracle in Yeats yield to the poet and man whose vision of the beast *truly* "troubles my sight."

This troubled vision is most subtly communicated in the greatest of Yeats's historical-apocalyptic poems—"Nineteen Hundred and Nineteen," in which the blank-eyed rough beast of "The Second Coming" appears as a blonde beast resembling Graves's "ignorant pale" rider. Yeats may have been both thrilled and troubled by his vision of the Sphinx-beast; he was merely appalled by his vision of that "insolent fiend Robert Artisson," the fourteenth-century incubus who corrupted the aristocratic Lady Kyteler and who, in the violent climax of Yeats's poem,

> lurches past, his great eyes *without thought*
> Under the shadow of *stupid straw-pale* locks.

Finally, the "Gusts of laughter" that stir the moon seem Yeatsian as well: an echo of the destruction-loving Nietzschean laughter in "The Gyres," the last of Yeats's apocalyptic poems. There, too, as in "The Destroyers," despite the coarse debasement of values at present, the return of a greater and "more gracious" dispensation is predicted. Though "Hector is dead and there's a light in Troy, / We that look on but laugh in tragic joy."[54] Those initiated into the mysteries of the whirling gyres can even ask (in an image that puts the beast in the saddle): "What matter though numb nightmare ride on top?"[55] This is temporarily tolerable because, inevitably, the old "noble" order of beauty, refinement, and "worth" shall return,

> and all things run
> On that unfashionable gyre again.

Though the Yeatsian turn of the wheel brings back lovers of women and craftsmen, what returns is a patriarchal aristocracy; the Gravesian return is matriarchal. In "The Destroyers"—as in "The Second Coming," "Nineteen Hundred and Nineteen," and "The Gyres"—a form of Dionysian-instinctual energy returns to overturn an imposed Apollonian-intellectual order. But in Graves's poem it is the Goddess who destroys the destroyers: that aristocracy of male conquerors that corrupted her Bassarids, despoiled the fertile "fields," and "Let the central hearth grow cold." But this hearth, rekindled, is a matriarchal center that *will* hold. However closely related to the historical supplanting of a matriarchal-agricultural by a patriarchal-military order, this imagery evokes as well timeless moral realities. For, as Kirkham has said,

> the 'central hearth' and the 'fields' are, symbolically, the inner life ('central' in that sense, too) of instinct, spiritual truth and reverence, as opposed to intellect in the service of greed and the 'arbitrary male will.' And still the Laura Riding ethic is at the centre of Graves's attitudes. Her actual words perhaps are echoed here, for in *The World and Ourselves* she states what is in fact the theme of the poem: 'a confused outer brutality envelops the inner hearth of life where we cultivate all that we know to be precious and true.'[56]

As we have seen, for Riding and Graves, Yeats was part of the confused brutality threatening what they knew to be "precious and true." But disagreement hardly prevents a poet from using, and abusing, a precursor. Different readers will feel differently about this proposed network of echoes or analogies. For me, at the end of "The Destroyers," with the return of the suppressed imminent, a remarkably Yeatsian rough beast is employed to slouch to the long-omitted feast of a lunar Goddess. Vengeful and sardonic, she is stirred by icy "Gusts of laughter" because it is *her* postponed hour that has come round at last; and it will be, as (interestingly enough) Yeats put it in the title of his sole poem about Perseus, "Her Triumph."

*   *   *   *

Is it all occult mummery; or do Graves and Yeats have sophisticated doubts about their own deterministic cycles of history and of individual experience? And in their shared passion to recover hidden "truth," how cavalier can they afford to be with mere external "facts"—or with common humanity? Of Graves, George Steiner has said, "In no man is the part of imagination harnessed more tightly to that of reason and argument."[57] True; but when Graves seems caught up in his own phantasmagoria—when we hear the monotonous chant of Kill! and Blood! or the cold but perhaps even crueler gusts of laughter that stir the ultimately victorious lunar Goddess—where then is the civility that tempers wildness?

Fortunately, both Graves and Yeats are double-minded men. Describing the genesis of their respective mythographic studies, they use similar language. Yeats was "overwhelmed by miracle"; Graves experienced "a sudden overwhelming obsession."[58] But each is capable as well of rational recovery. They may succumb and recover in virtually the same moment. The disciplined control of even the most violent poems suggests the tight-harnessing to which Steiner refers. There is no need to illustrate the obvious: Graves's persistent emphasis on formal craft and intellectual lucidity; look, for example, at the interwoven pattern of end and internal rhymes in the ostensibly wild final stanza of "The Destroyers." The same control is evident in Yeats. The whirling tumult of images in the final movement of "Nineteen Hundred and Nineteen" is conveyed in rhymed pentameters; "Leda and the Swan" cunningly merges elements of the Shakespearean and Petrarchan sonnet; the Hysterica passio of "The Gyres" and of "Her Vision in the Wood" is held down by ceremonious ottava rima. The more violent the content, the more severely disciplined the restraining form, as in *The Bacchae* of Euripides.

At other times, the rational recovery, and the consequent note of urbane skepticism, is itself held down—or at least held back from the reader. Yeats and Graves both let a dozen years pass before they admitted unmistakable caveats into the public texts of *A Vision* and *The White Goddess*.

We are told by Yeats in the introduction to the 1937 version of *A Vision* that the spirits who allegedly spoke through his wife advised him not to spend his life pondering their metaphysics. In a happy reciprocity, he was to give "concrete expression to their abstract thought": thought that was to be embodied, for they had "come to give you metaphors for poetry." And the concluding words of that introduction amount to an extended disclaimer:

> Some will ask whether I believe in the actual existence of my circuits of sun and moon. . . . To such a question I can but answer that if sometimes, overwhelmed by miracle as all men must be when in the midst of it, I have taken such periods literally, my reason has soon recovered; and now that the system stands out clearly in my imagination I regard them as stylistic arrangements of experience comparable to the cubes in the drawing of Wyndham Lewis and to the ovoids in the sculpture of Brancusi. They have helped me to hold in a single thought reality and justice.[59]

Acknowledging that much if not all of *A Vision* imposes a just but fictive symmetry upon the chaos of the actual, Yeats opens the definitive version of that book by sharing with us his rather urbane skepticism regarding its contents. Graves advances his argument as if he were trafficking not only with truth but also with *the* truth. Not until the postscript, added (as Yeats's introduction was) a dozen years after the original publication of the book, are we granted a glimpse behind the mask of the learned rhapsode who composed *The White Goddess*. Before turning to that postscript, we might synopsize critical response to Graves's Goddess.

There are those who dismiss the Goddess as irrelevant (Fraser) or diminish her as a psychological projection, specifically a surrogate for Laura Riding (Jarrell), or deplore her as a doleful return to Romanticism (Cohen). The central critics (Day, Kirkham, Hoffman) see her as a mixture of psychic and larger mythical truth. Mehoke, who, along with Vickery, takes the mythopoeia most seriously, argues that the view that "the alert reader may find the myth unnecessary" (Hoffman) or that "the Myth recedes into the background for a majority of the poems" (Kirkham) emphasizes "individual poems and readings," while his own presentation "attempts to emphasize connections and relations with the Myth and within the poetry as an inseparable whole."[60]

Since I too emphasize interaction, such an integrating approach is congenial; but I find it just as difficult to accept Graves's Goddess worship without qualification as I do to accept, as some Yeatsian critics do, Yeats's "Neoplatonism." The poets themselves tend to treat these matters discreetly. Even when, like Yeats and Graves, they produce prose codifications of the myth, they prefer not to look too deeply into the mouth of the gift horse who brings them their metaphors for poetry.

Of course, certain elements in the genesis of the Goddess are unmistakable. In personal terms, she embodies Graves's preference for his gemütlich mother to his father, and he has always been attracted to dominant women: Nancy Nicholson, Laura Riding. (Along with the Goddess herself, he has created one of the most formidable heroines in literary history in Livia, the murderous but dedicated Roman matriarch of *I, Claudius*.) At the same time, as Day has observed, Graves was "brought up on the algolagnic heroines of Swinburne, the wan, hypnotic beauties of the Romantic poets, and the Fatal Women of Elizabethan tragedy; and his vision of the Goddess corresponds so closely to these stereotypes that it is impossible to see her solely as the product of his personal experiences."[61]

She is, in fact, experience mythologized and myth made personal. On the mythographic level, the Sacred King is "the Moon-goddess's divine victim," and "every Muse-poet must, in a sense, die for the Goddess whom he adores, just as the King died." Thus, on the individual level, "being in love does not, and should not, blind the poet to the cruel side of woman's nature—and many Muse-poems are written in helpless attestation of this by men whose love is no longer returned" (*WG*, pp. 489, 491).

It seems accurate to say that Graves has, in describing the White Goddess, woven "an always personal emotion . . . into a general pattern of myth and symbol." I am quoting Yeats (*Autobiography*, pp. 101–2); once again, it is he who provides the most striking parallel with Graves. Both poets tend to submit themselves to dominant women; and both, as poets in the Anglo-Irish tradition, know all about the fairy mistress called the "Leanhaun Shee." This "malignant," vampirish phantom is "the Gaelic Muse, for she gives inspiration to those she persecutes. . . . To her have belonged the greatest of the Irish poets, from Oisin down to the last century."[62] In his earliest poems, even before he had met that statuesque embodiment of the femme fatale, Maud Gonne, Yeats was writing poems (*The Island of Statues*, *The Two Titans*, *The Seeker*) that are part of the Romantic agony of submission to the merciless belle dames, the fatal enchantresses and dominating earth and sea mothers, of Romanticism.

What the poets *believe* about all this is another matter. Though he admires *Swifter than Reason*, Christopher Ricks concludes that Day "does rather shirk the question of whether or not we need to believe all that about the White Goddess, and even whether or not Graves really believes it."[63] But even Mehoke, ostensibly a true believer, opens the final paragraph of his book with a question and a tentative response: "Does Graves really believe in his laboriously constructed vision? Perhaps he does, just as each of us believes his own kind of 'vision' of how things 'are.' " This is more affirmative than Day's dismissal ("whether or not Graves believes in her as a true Goddess is irrelevant"); but, as Monroe K. Spears has noted, "it would seem, rather, to be extremely relevant, though difficult, to try to define the exact nature of Graves's belief in this divinity, the ontological status that he conceives her to occupy."[64]

The triple distinction between the actual existence of the Goddess as a supernatural being, belief in such a deity, and the effects of such belief, is taken up in the previously mentioned 1960 postscript to *The White Goddess*. There, repeating much of what he'd said in a 1957 lecture on the book's genesis, Graves tells of a series of more-than-coincidental happenings attending his discovery of the Goddess, events that seem examples of Jungian synchronicity. He would call them, Graves says, "supernatural hauntings" but for his aversion to that adjective; and in any case he finds such occurrences natural enough, though "superlatively unscientific." Continuing this scientific-unscientific distinction, he remarks that though no god at all can be scientifically proved to exist ("only beliefs in gods, and the effects of such beliefs on worshippers"), most scientists, as products of a patriarchal culture, are "God-worshippers." As for himself,

> I cannot make out why a belief in a Father-god's authorship of the universe, and its laws, seems any less unscientific than a belief in a Mother-goddess's inspiration of this artificial system. Granted the first metaphor, the second follows logically—if these *are* no better than metaphors. (*WG*, p. 490)

The implication is that they *are* better than metaphors; but the convoluted formulation ("seems any less unscientific") is revealing, and both the reference to "metaphor" and the "if" are resonant. A moment later he adds:

> Since the source of poetry's creative power is not scientific intelligence, but inspiration—however this may be explained by scientists—one may surely attribute inspiration to the Lunar Muse, the oldest and most convenient European term for this source? (*WG*, p. 490)

Quite aside from the blasé rhetorical question (a form of answer that simultaneously asks), the pragmatic vocabulary—"most convenient . . . term"—has suddenly become that of the detached comparative mythologist. The Goddess may abide, but her ontological status seems undermined. In the lecture on which the postscript is based, Graves treated the matter of his "literal" inspiration by the White Goddess even more gingerly. It is, he told his YM-YWHA audience, an "improper" question—just as it would be improper for him to ask them if the Hebrew prophets were "literally inspired" by God. "Whether God is a metaphor or a fact cannot be reasonably argued: let us likewise be discreet on the subject of the Goddess" (*OP*, p. 242)

In this same lecture, Graves first advanced (in a form in which he allowed himself considerable latitude) what was to become the most direct statement of position in the postscript. He said of himself in the lecture: "I am no mystic. I studiously avoid witchcraft, spiritualism, Yoga, fortune-telling, automatic writing, and so on." This catalog, like the similar catalog in the final section of Eliot's "The Dry Salvages," amounts to another slap at Yeats. But whatever his fascination with the occult, Yeats might have answered (as he did in a letter to Ethel Mannin written a month before his death): "Am I a mystic?—no, I am a practical man. I have seen the raising of Lazarus and the loaves and fishes and have made the usual measurements, plummet line, spirit-level and have taken the temperature by pure mathematic."[65]

But we have interrupted Graves. He continues, sounding now rather like the domestic Yeats of "What Then?" ("A small old house, wife, daughter, son, / . . . / Poets and wits about him drew"):

> I live a simple, normal, rustic life with my wife, my children, and a wide circle of sane and intelligent friends. I belong to no religious cult, no secret society, no philosophic sect; but I do value my historical intuition, which I trust up to the point where it can be factually checked.

When this passage was repeated, almost verbatim, in the postscript to *The White Goddess*, the one substantial alteration was in the final phrase. The originally positive formulation ("but I *do* value") yielded to a more carefully qualified assertion that begins negatively: "*nor* do I trust my historical intuition any further than it can be factually checked" (*WG*, p. 488).

Though, as the lecturer engagingly asked his audience, "There's nothing so strange about that?" (an "asking"-answer omitted in the postscript), his methodology marks him as poet rather than historian. In both formulations, however qualified, emphasis is placed on poetic "intuition." Though Graves's terminology provides a patina of science, his use of proleptic and analeptic methods of suspending time so as to anticipate or recover hidden truth makes for an intuitive-comparative methodology considerably more speculative than that of either trained historians or Frazer and the Cambridge school of anthropologizing classicists.

With reason yielding to imagination and intuition, double-minded Graves cannot be said to owe his "historical method" to great-granduncle von Ranke. He is a poet; and whatever Graves's zeal to disclose hidden truth, whatever his contempt for poets (preeminently Yeats) who lack "integrity" and a comparable will to truth, the Zarathustra quoted by Yeats seems accurate: "we poets lie too much." Recently, Laura Riding, attacking Graves's "transmogrifications of my thinking, draped with costumery from the bulging wardrobe of literary myth lore," has belittled *The White Goddess*, a book of "sham religiosity," as his "most intricately truthless" production.[66]

But whatever the ambiguities of the situation, including Laura Riding's subsequent disclaimer of any "involvement in a poker-faced muse or goddess game of poetic didactics," Graves's method of intuitive time-suspension does lead him to a Goddess whose presence has unmistakably enriched his work. The key text here is the short poem "On Portents," which is, as Kirkham suggests, "the first fully-fledged White Goddess poem" (p. 142). We can approach "On Portents" by observing that the distinction we have been tracing between historical and "intuitive" method is akin to Graves's distinction, fiercely maintained, between the prosaic and the poetic. "What interests me most in conducting this argument," he says midway through *The White Goddess*, "is the difference that is constantly appearing between the poetic and prosaic methods of thought." The prosaic method, he sensibly contends, "was invented by the Greeks of the Classical age as an insurance against the swamping of reason by mythographic fancy." But what began as insurance has hardened into orthodoxy: "single-strand prose" as "the only legitimate means of transmitting useful knowledge." As a result, except in those rare individuals who "privately struggle to cultivate it," the "poetic faculty is atrophied" (*WG*, p. 223).

That faculty is not, however, atrophied in the feminine mind, which, properly cultivated, is unaffected by history, always capable of that suspension of time that indicates the presence of the White Goddess. She can speak through a man, whether Robert Graves or Caliban—to whom Shakespeare gives "the truest poetry" of *The Tempest* precisely because his mother, the witch Sycorax, *is* the White Goddess, here making "her last appearance in the plays." Citing Caliban's lines beginning "Be not afeard: the isle is full of noises" (3. 2. 131–40), Graves notes that the "illogical sequence of tenses creates a perfect suspension of time" (*WG*, pp. 426–27). And in a poem he pays the tribute of "loving admiration" to a woman who, journeying with difficulty "Through nightmare to a lost and moated land," dreams herself into a place beyond all dream. There, in certain rare and privileged moments, she will find herself seated among a visionary company:

> The untameable, the live, the gentle.
> Have you not known them? Whom? They carry
> Time looped so river-wise about their house
> There's no way in by history's road
> To name or number them.

"Any unspoilt woman," said Graves in 1970, "is capable of using her mind in the timeless, nonchalant way characteristic of genius: which is to make extraordinary complicated problems seem as simple as counting one's fingers—by the manipulation of time." After quoting "On Portents," which was written "of a woman genius," he adds: "In real love, as opposed to confused sexual groping or a simple decision to marry and settle down, genius is always present; and manifests itself with its usual suprasensory binding of time into a manageable ring."[67]

So the hauntingly beautiful lines from "Through Nightmare" about time looped river-wise constitute a gentler, more "civilized" version of the conquest of time and linear history in "On Portents"—a poem in which the timelessness of the theme, the suspension of time in the poetic act, and the superiority of the Goddess to that element all come together. One of the very few poems of his own that Graves admits into *The White Goddess*, "On Portents" is used in that context to illustrate an extension of the doctrine of proleptic thought: that, "in the poetic act, time is suspended and details of future experience often become incorporated in the poem, as they do in dreams" (*WG*, p. 343). Beginning with this markedly Yeatsian precursor of the theme poems, our next section will move toward those poems in which the Goddess makes her major appearances.

V

> If strange things happen where she is,
> So that men say that graves open
> And the dead walk, or that futurity
> Becomes a womb and the unborn are shed,
> Such portents are not to be wondered at,
> Being tourbillions in Time made
> By the strong pulling of her bladed mind
> Through that ever-reluctant element.

The "she" of "On Portents" reflects the Isis of Apuleius and of Plutarch, whose "On Isis and Osiris" Graves was reading during the period of the poem's composition (1929–1931). She also, as J. M. Cohen has observed (p. 64), "shares with Yeats's Maud Gonne the capacity for disturbing history." This will draw no argument from readers of, say, "No Second Troy," where Yeats's Helen—no more "to be wondered at" than Graves's Goddess—is absolved of all blame for her "violent ways" in a passage that may have suggested one element of the weaponlike mind, and perhaps even Graves's syntactical construction pivoting on "Being":

> What could have made her peaceful with a mind
> That nobleness made simple as a fire,
> With beauty like a tightened bow, a kind
> That is not natural in an age like this,
> Being high and solitary and most stern?

But "On Portents" may be still more Yeatsian. Graves's curious image of gyrelike "tourbillions" made by cutting through time recalls a curious image employed by Yeats in another of his celebrations of a strong woman, in this case Augusta Gregory. Yeats describes, as a less violent but equally irresistible strong pulling, the capacity of that "woman's powerful character" to keep her literary acolytes in concentrated formation, so that, seeming "to whirl upon a compass-point," they found

> certainty upon the dreaming air,
> The intellectual sweetness of those lines
> That cut through time or cross it withershins.

The possibility that Graves may have been familiar with the poem (first published in 1931) is enhanced by the presence of what seems to be a variation on the Yeatsian image in Graves's "The Felloe'd Year," the thematic twin of "On Portents." There, the poet, admitting that he is caught up in the "creak and groan" of the painfully turning wheel of the seasons in which all still move, prays that "the twelve spokes of this round felloe'd year / Be a fixed compass, not a turning wheel."

Though it is an "ever-reluctant element," time is of a most equivocal nature. It can be suspended—fixed upon a compass point—by the poet in the act of creation, the poet's work being done, as Blake says, in the momentary pulsation of an artery, in what Wordsworth calls a spot of time. More violently, it can be cut through by the propellerlike mind of the "woman genius" or of the Muse Goddess herself, whose symbol is the double-bladed ax. Or it can be crossed in a contrariwise direction—"withershins," in Yeats's word, a word known to Graves, who tells us of a witch charged with "dancing widdershins" around men's houses while stark naked, a tourbillion that "portended ill-luck" (*WG*, p. 445). And, thanks to a book that both poets studied closely in 1931, time can be demonstrated to be "not the stable moving-staircase that prose-men have for centuries pretended it to be, but an unaccountable wibble-wobble" (to quote Graves's synopsis of J. W. Dunne's *Experiments with Time* in support of what is said about time in "On Portents").[68] The Mad Hatter's tea party still goes on.

This conception of time as a wibble-wobble—an unsteady, alternating zigzag—accords with Graves's penchant for flying crooked. Yet in "The Felloe'd Year" (a strong poem unaccountably never reprinted after its first appearance), he acknowledges his Ixion-like bondage and is reduced to "praying" that he be exempted from the inexorable turning of the temporal wheel, that the seasonal and zodiacal spokes of the year might radiate inward to a fixed compass point rather than outward to the wheel's necessarily restricting rim. In Romantic poetry, the shattering of the prose-men's conception of time as stable often takes the form of a radical conflation. We hear of "the Bard who present, past, & future sees" (Blake); of "Ancestral voices prophesying war" (Coleridge); of "what is past, or passing, or to come" (Yeats). In "On Portents," Graves's analeptic and proleptic methods of thought coalesce in a suspended present in which "graves open / And the dead walk," while, simultaneously, "futurity / Becomes a womb and the unborn are shed." Complete triumph over time, in occult and Romantic texts alike, tends to take the form of an inward whirling to a centripetal center. In the hero's initiatory purification in Graves's "Instructions to the Orphic Adept," one of his most rhythmically compelling performances, we return to such a still point. Completion of the ritual takes man "Out of the weary wheel, the

71

circling years, / To that still, spokeless wheel:—Persephone."

For both Graves and Yeats, the power to make her chosen men "perne in a gyre" is possessed only by woman—in Graves's case, the Muse Goddess, in her various mythological forms or as incarnate in a mortal woman; for Yeats, as resident in the tourbillion Maud Gonne (or, as in "Coole Park, 1929," in the sweet disciplinarian Augusta Gregory). Always present are the elements of discipline, compulsion, and the devotee's persistent effort throughout the exacting ordeal. The Orphic initiate must, for example, be able to answer the climactic question by emphasizing his own effort in the required submission: "My feet have borne me here." Above all, man must submit to woman's judgment. In the "fundamental relation," which is between male and female mind, "the female mind is the judge, and the male mind the subject of judgment." Thus spake Laura Riding, the "woman genius" Graves had in mind when he wrote "On Portents."[69] This seems tyrannous; but then, as Lucius says of Isis in *The Golden Ass* (which Graves thinks the fullest depiction of the Goddess in literature), "Her service is perfect freedom." Resenting St. Augustine's Christian cribbing from Apuleius and his application of the phrase to "the ideally benign Father-god" (*WG*, p. 485), Graves has made Lucius's address his motto and transformed Isis into his own Goddess.

It is significant that "On Portents," so proleptic of Graves's future direction, was placed in the fifth and final section of the 1938 *Collected Poems*, part of a small group of lyrics that, according to Graves's foreword, express "a more immediate sense of poetic liberation"—though it is a liberation "achieved," Graves adds, "not by mysticism but by practical persistence" (p. xiii). In "On Portents," that persistence takes the form, first, of the Goddess's own efforts to overcome resistance. But it is the poet-lover who is caught up in the turbulence made by the strong pulling of her bladed mind. Clearly, service to the Goddess—then incarnate in Laura Riding, who had as bladed a mind as even Graves could wish—must take the form of a freedom to be achieved only after considerable difficulty, and pain, on the part of her acolyte.

The more-than-metaphoric significance of that "bladed" mind is stressed in the final stanza of "End of Play," in this same concluding section of the 1938 *Collected Poems*. At the end of "pastime" (presided over by a "foolish smiling Mary-mantle blue" sky), childish illusions are put away by those who have ceased idling and—that familiar imperative—"tell no lies now." Gone is the shallow faith of weaklings who, "on their knees / Call lugubriously upon chaste Christ." So much for Christianity, including Mariolatry, about which Graves is usually less severe; that it is St. Paul who is echoed in this putting away of the things of a child is, of course, a typically Gravesian irony. Gone too are both "hypocritic pomp" and "bestial sensuality," with its "frantic laceration of naked breasts."

> Yet love survives, the word carved on a sill
> Under antique dread of the headsman's axe;
> It is the echoing mind, as in the mirror
> We stare at our dazed trunks at the block kneeling.

The awestruck, and imaginatively posthumous, affirmation of love's survival even of the block seems very different in tone from the brusque dismissal of the Christian order with its sentimentalities and dichotomies. Yet the final stanza gathers up the echo-and-mirror imagery of stanza 2—"a mirror and an echo / Mediate henceforth with vision and sound"—and the final effect is one of change within a deeper continuity. The old faith and the old self (equally deluded, childish, idling, mendacious, "romantic") have died; the new, more "mettlesome" faith and self are born—only to be instantly subjected to the ax of an unsentimental, fiercer romanticism. Though this constitutes a new vision, it is revealed, like most things ostensibly new, to be "antique," the adjective Graves later reserves for the "antique story" told in *The White Goddess* (*WG*, p. 24). In the imaginative mirror that now mediates that newly reconstructed vision of martyrdom, we stare at our own dazed trunks, victims kneeling in adoration. In Graves as in Yeats, "stare" is part of the vocabulary of the sublime, a verb expressing stunned wonder and, as here, pulsing with daemonic, bloody potential. The primal scene established in these lines will become standard in Graves's mythology; for this is decapitation by a headsman proleptic of the White Goddess: that archetypal ax-wielder whose bladed mind pulls strongly deep in our own, or at least in Robert Graves's, "echoing mind."

The replacement of the childish viewpoint, again reduced to delusion ("These were all lies"), by a now austere vision is most dramatically embodied in "A Love Story," the masterful opening poem of Graves's next volume. The delusive spring and relentless winter of that poem are then transformed to a genuine midwinter spring in a poem in which the Muse Goddess revives her poet from hibernation ("Mid-Winter Waking," 1939). And the Goddess herself finally appears in all her terrible beauty in three of Graves's most hypnotic, resonant hymns: "To Juan at the Winter Solstice," "Darien," and the quest poem entitled "The White Goddess," where, recalling the mirror and echo of "End of Play," she is called "Sister of the mirage and echo."

"A Love Story" opens theatrically on a symbolic winter moonscape, introduces a reflexively urbane note, then returns to the sublime and a "shiver" as complex as the "shivering glory" of "Sick Love."[70]

> The full moon easterly rising, furious,
> Against a winter sky ragged with red;
> The hedges high in snow, and owls raving—
> Solemnities not easy to withstand:
> A shiver wakes the spine.

The double nature of that shiver, compounded of terror and longing, is developed in the rest of the poem: a fantasia of recollection that moves from boyhood fear through illusory fulfillment of longing to the revelation that the speaker has been the victim of a dangerous deception, fundamentally self-deception. The poem ends on a note that, precisely because it is so perfectly disciplined, suggests temporary quietude rather than permanent paralysis:

In boyhood, having encountered the scene,
I suffered horror: I fetched the moon home,
With owls and snow, to nurse in my head
Throughout the trials of a new Spring,
Famine unassuaged.

But fell in love, and made a lodgement
Of love on those chill ramparts.
Her image was my ensign: snows melted,
Hedges sprouted, the moon tenderly shone,
The owls trilled with tongues of nightingale.

These were all lies, though they matched the time,
And brought me less than luck: her image
Warped in the weather, turned beldamish.
Then back came winter on me at a bound,
The pallid sky heaved with a moon-quake.

Dangerous it had been with love-notes
To serenade Queen Famine.
In tears I recomposed the former scene,
Let the snow lie, watched the moon rise, suffered the owls,
Paid homage to them of unevent.

The stage properties and the final inaction suggest a reworking of an earlier poem we have already glanced at. "Full Moon" also has owl and nightingale and a moon that, "attained to her full height," presides over the "defeat" of lovers who "held the tyrannous moon above / Sole mover of their fate." Both "queens" adumbrate the archetype, Queen Famine being the White Goddess in her malevolent, ravenous aspect. Just as the young man's sexual and emotional hunger is "unassuaged," so the incarnate queen, in satisfying her need to seduce, whets her appetite for vengeance on the deluded lover whose ensign was her image, bringing him, in Graves's marvelous meiosis, "less than luck."

The vengeance is cruel but, in part at least, justified by his mixture of naiveté and presumption, and by his subsequent complaining. He has been, as Graves would later say, "party to his own betrayal and has no just cause for complaint" (*WG*, p. 448). The young man's folly in making a "lodgement / Of love on those chill ramparts" is revealed not only in the difficult, precarious, and frigid nature of such a lodgement, but in the insipidity and unnaturalness of snow melting in winter, hedges sprouting, and owls trilling. This, as Kirkham says, is "the poet's sardonic judgment" on the lover's "mistaking a temporary phase of sanguine romanticism for the full reality" of the man-woman relationship, which is in truth a "constantly changing cycle of situations" (pp. 190, 189). The Gravesian speaker should admit, as he does in a related poem ("To Sleep"), "Loving in part, I did not see you whole."

When her image, warping in the weather, "turned beldamish" (that is, like a hideous old woman, but with a play on *la belle dame sans merci*), the winter that the lover dreamed transformed by love comes "back" on him at a predatory "bound." In his tearful recomposition of the former scene, the tragic wintry bleakness is restored: he let the snow "lie" (unmelted, truthfully inert), "watched the moon rise" ("furious," as it had been at the outset, not domesticated and shining "tenderly"), and "suffered the owls" (enduring their screech, rather than imagining it changed to the romantic song of the nightingale).

In the middle phase, her lunar image had been his ensign; now the "homage" paid to moon, owls, and snow (earlier "nursed" and sentimentally softened in his head) is the passivity of "unevent." It may seem that the death of love in the present (the first and last stanzas) has returned the man, regressively, to the stage of boyhood with its horror of love. But in fact he has advanced, attaining a sort of Wordsworthian sober maturity. In the final lunar phase, coming again to the terrifying scene he encountered as a boy, he knows the place for the first time. He has moved beyond inexperienced dread, delusion, and the hubristic serenading of Queen Famine with facile love notes. Now the poet-lover simply submits, chastened and resigned to his fate as vassal of the moon goddess whose service, Graves will soon announce, is perfect freedom. His homage is of unevent; but there is such a thing as wise (if sad) passiveness, and of course they also serve who only stand and wait. The readiness is all: Graves, examining his own aging face in the mirror, is soon to ask himself why "He still stands ready, with a boy's presumption, / To court the queen in her high silk pavilion" ("The Face in the Mirror"). But the man knows what the boy didn't: the precariousness of that courtship of the Muse.

The compensation and reward for waiting in readiness, one eye open, come in the revivification of "Mid-Winter Waking," a beautiful love lyric and Muse-poet poem with Keatsian echoes:

> Stirring suddenly from long hibernation,
> I knew myself once more a poet
> Guarded by timeless principalities
> Against the worm of death, this hillside haunting;
> And presently dared open both my eyes.

The ambiguity of the syntax allows us to read "this hillside haunting" as referring to either the speaker or "the worm of death." Either way, we are reminded of Keats's dreaming knight-at-arms who, guarded by "pale kings and princes," "awoke and found me here / On the cold hill's side." But in Graves's "waking" (quite different from the knight's, and from the shiver that "wakes" the spine in "A Love Story"), there is union, not abandonment, and, rather than isolated "unevent," the shared event of a true love story.

The remaining two stanzas are gratefully addressed to the mysterious powers of inspiration at the back of the mind and to their external manifestation in "sudden warm airs," winter's harbingers of the fruitful spring to come:

> O gracious, lofty, shone against from under,
> Back-of-the-mind-far clouds like towers;
> And you, sudden warm airs that blow
> Before the expected season of new blossom,
> While sheep still gnaw at roots and lambless go—
>
> Be witness that on waking, this mid-winter,
> I found her hand in mine laid closely
> Who shall watch out the Spring with me.
> We stared in silence all around us
> But found no winter anywhere to see.

For the conclusion of his poem "Her Triumph," with its sudden revelation and liberation brought by love—"And now we stare astonished at the sea / And a miraculous strange bird shrieks at us"—Yeats turned to the conclusion of the sonnet in which Keats, on first looking into Chapman's Homer, felt like Cortez

> when with eagle eyes
> He stared at the Pacific—and all his men
> Looked at each other with a wild surmise—
> Silent, upon a peak in Darien.

Graves, who took the name of his Goddess's son, Darien, from this sonnet, also alludes to these lines—to better effect than Yeats—in the conclusion of "Mid-Winter Waking": "We stared in silence all around us / But found no winter anywhere to see."

Later in this section of *Collected Poems*, in an exquisite short lyric that combines eternally springing hope and plangent elegy, Graves offers his unimprovable final word on signs of spring in winter:

> She tells her love while half asleep,
> In the dark hours,
> With half-words whispered low:
> As Earth stirs in her winter sleep
> And puts out grass and flowers
> Despite the snow,
> Despite the falling snow.

The poem first appeared, as a song Orpheus sings of the dead Eurydice, in Graves's *The Golden Fleece*, the novel he was working on when he was suddenly overwhelmed by the figure of the White Goddess. We turn now to the poems in which she appears, the poems specifically designated by Graves as "Magical."

Randall Jarrell finds these "mythical-archaic" pieces Graves's "richest, most moving, and most consistently beautiful poems—poems that almost deserve the literal *magical.* . . . The best of these are different from anything else in English" (*The Third Book of Criticism*, pp. 90–91). Before discussing the three most representative of these poems, it may be useful to have Graves's own synopsis of his Muse and her myth.

Whatever her roots in, and reflections of, Graves's own

biography and psyche, his Goddess seems essentially an extension of two Romantic concerns. One is the sublime. "The function of poetry," writes Graves, "is religious invocation of the Muse; its use is the experience of mixed exaltation and horror that her presence excites" (*WG*, p. 14). The other is the submission to the femme fatale: a poet, even the nineteenth-century Romantic, was, says Graves, "a true poet only in his fatalistic regard for the Goddess as the mistress who commanded his destiny" (*WG*, p. 25). That Graves has in mind particularly the author of "La Belle Dame sans Merci" and his Muse, Fanny Brawne, is suggested in the conclusion of his most succinct synopsis of the theme:

> The Theme, briefly, is the antique story . . . of the birth, life, death and resurrection of the God of the Waxing Year; the central chapters concern the God's losing battle with the God of the Waning Year for love of the capricious and all-powerful Threefold Goddess, their mother, bride, and layer-out. The poet identifies himself with the God of the Waxing Year and his Muse with the Goddess. . . . All true poetry—true by Housman's practical test—celebrates some incident or scene in this very ancient story.

Housman's famous test of a true poem was that the hair bristles if one repeats it while shaving. Housman didn't explain *why*; Graves does:

> The reason why the hairs stand on end, the eyes water, the throat is constricted, the skin crawls and a shiver runs down the spine when one writes or reads a true poem is that a true poem is necessarily an invocation of the White Goddess, or Muse, the Mother of All Living, the ancient power of fright and lust—the female spider or the queen-bee whose embrace is death. Housman offered a secondary test of true poetry: whether it matches a phrase of Keats's, "everything that reminds me of her goes through me like a spear." This is equally pertinent to the Theme. Keats was writing under the shadow of death about his Muse, Fanny Brawne; and the "spear that roars for blood" is the traditional weapon of the dark executioner and supplanter. (*WG*, pp. 24–25)

Execution and supplanting are the inevitable denouement; but Graves, counting the beats of his single theme, covers a considerable spectrum. The Goddess is at her most terrible in "The Destroyers" and the even more sardonic "Dethronement" (dropped in 1965), in which the lover's "true anguish / Is all that she requires." She is at her most winning, for me, as Ariadne, in that splendid exposure of male egotism and self-deception, "Theseus and Ariadne," which ends with the deserted woman a triumphant moon goddess, "Playing the queen" to the "nobler company" of the lover who succeeded ignorant Theseus when he abandoned her on Naxos: the god Dionysus.

In between are those central demonstrations of Graves's wild civility, the poems in which the Goddess is both terrible and beautiful. It is not necessary to reproduce the elaborate glosses, by Graves and others, that have accumulated around the best known of these—the best known, indeed, of all Graves's poems. The critic's function in discussing "To Juan at the Winter Solstice" is, in fact, largely reduced to annotation, a flaw in the poem if judged by Graves's own criterion: plain expression requiring no "learned" glosses. As an epitomization of *The White Goddess*, the poem provides a remarkable synopsis of its "antique story" of the solar hero's relationship with the Triple Goddess, his union with her, and his inevitable death at her hands or by her command. Whatever stories his newborn son Juan may eventually tell—whether of trees, or beasts, or birds, or stars; of the Virgin compounded of Aphrodite and Rahab, or of Ophion, the "undying snake from chaos hatched"—it will always be the same story, to which

> all lines or lesser gauds belong
> That startle with their shining
> Such common stories as they stray into.

Like the son to whom the poem is addressed, we are preempted from originality. It's all in *The White Goddess*, with everything *not* there reduced by definition to the "common," brightened only by the fortuitous intermixture of stray threads from the monomyth. The truly "magical" thing about "To Juan at the Winter Solstice" is that, despite Graves's exclusive claim-staking and thematic reductiveness, the poem itself is a triumph of incantatory resonance. I will be suggesting that what the poem gains in the awestruck power of the sublime, it pays for in human terms. But first that power must be granted. Even the grimmest cyclical determinism, that governing the life-and-death cycle of the Goddess's consort, is made exultant, shot through as it is with the constellated light of the turning zodiac:

> Water to water, ark again to ark,
> From woman back to woman:
> So each new victim treads unfalteringly
> The never altered circuit of his fate,
> Bringing twelve peers as witness
> Both to his starry rise and starry fall.

To appreciate these lines it is not really necessary to know that solar heroes, traditionally born at the winter solstice, reappear in reincarnated form at that time, floating on a waterborne ark; nor that the "twelve peers"—like Christ's apostles and like knights Arthurian and French—personify the months of the year and the signs of the zodiac. Nor do we need glosses from *The White Goddess* on owl, elder tree, and Yule log in order to respond to the eerie power of the penultimate stanza:

> Much snow is falling, winds roar hollowly,
> The owl hoots from the elder,
> Fear in your heart cries to the loving-cup:
> Sorrow to sorrow as the sparks fly upward.
> The log groans and confesses:
> There is one story and one story only.

Following these death-haunted lines—their acceleration resolved in the finality of the repetition, "There is one story and one story only"—we are left to ponder the imponderable: the ambivalent threefold nature of the Goddess herself:

> Dwell on her graciousness, dwell on her smiling,
> Do not forget what flowers
> The great boar trampled down in ivy time.
> Her brow was creamy as the crested wave,
> Her sea-grey eyes were wild
> But nothing promised that is not performed.

Though Graves denied Eliot the right to mythopoeic conflation, taking him to task for inaccurately locating

Agamemnon's death in a bloody wood in "Sweeney Among the Nightingales," he does some conflating of his own here. The boar that killed so many solar heroes, among them Aphrodite's beloved, Adonis, is set trampling flowers at "ivy time"—that is, during October, which is both the boar-hunting season and the time of the revels of the Maenads. Frenzied priestesses of Dionysus, they chewed ivy as an intoxicant and would tear to pieces any man who interrupted their autumnal rites. No one who has read *The Bacchae*, and is here asked to "dwell on her graciousness, dwell on her smiling," is likely to forget the fate of Pentheus or Euripides' emphasis on the ever-smiling, inscrutable, destructive Dionysus.

Nevertheless, Juan is to dwell on this graciousness and smiling. The equivalent Yeatsian text is "A Prayer for My Daughter," in which the newborn child is advised to cultivate a kindlier beauty and to concentrate upon the gentler, more benign aspects of life. In both cases, the admonishing fathers acknowledge, implicitly or explicitly, their own fatal attraction to the fiercer aspects of that terrible beauty they join in celebrating. But where Yeats ends, as Coleridge does in "Frost at Midnight," with a prayer that his child enjoy a very different and serene fate, Graves's inexorable myth presses him to warn his son that whatever aspect of the Goddess he may concentrate on, she will inevitably turn as murderous as the Maenads. Yet, at the same time, she remains beautiful—creamy-browed and with eyes that, like la belle dame's, "were wild." "But" (and this is the final turn in the poem) everything that has been promised will be performed. During the time of allotted union, she shall bring her devotee love and inspiration—until the time comes for the ax to fall, as fall it must. Hence the negative construction of the final affirmation: "nothing promised that is not performed."

The Goddess is exacting, but just. She is also irresistible—an Aphrodite holding forth the promise both of sensuous bliss and of an experience that can end in only one way. There are no surprises, in either the myth or the poem: her graciousness and smiling are marked as ambivalent and fatal back in the central stanza. There, after being depicted both as a virgin, pure in her celestial "silver beauty," and as promiscuously sublunar, even subhuman ("all fish below the thighs"), she appears in an iconographic pose, gesturing, "her lips curved" (to quote "Rhea," another Goddess-poem) "In a half-smile archaic":

> She in her left hand bears a leafy quince;
> When with her right she crooks a finger, smiling,
> How may the King hold back?
> Royally then he barters life for love.

If we let the poem do its work, the bargain with the Goddess seems worth it; we may suspend disbelief in the myth and allow Graves's architectural skill, the magnificence of his imagery and hypnagogic rhythms, to persuade us that he has made the vicissitudes of the man-woman relationship into "something like a Mystery play, which gives ritual shape to the varied incidents of a love story"; that "all the painfulness of love is here but impersonalized by its association with the full conception of love's meaning embodied in the Myth—of which suffering is only a necessary part" (Kirkham, p. 202). This is to see the sacred drama as, ultimately, a divine comedy in which individual agony is subsumed. Just such a ritual shaping and distancing occur in stanza 4 of the "Ode on a Grecian Urn." But Keats never forgets that what he is describing is a "sacrifice." He depicts the protesting victim (though it is merely a heifer) as "lowing at the skies," and makes the stanza end in full recognition of the "desolate" human consequences of participation in the sacrificial rite.

Similarly, in a poem no less dependent on the mythology behind it than "To Juan at the Winter Solstice," Yeats's "Byzantium," the ritualistic "dying into a dance" is yet described as "an agony." And the poem ends in emotional perplexity. The golden smithies of the Emperor and marbles of the dancing floor—emblems of the endorsed ritual of Byzantine "simplicity" and of the artifice of eternity—are twice said to "break" the flood of blood-begotten, unpurged spirits surging into the Holy City. They

> Break bitter furies of complexity,
> Those images that yet
> Fresh images beget,
> That dolphin-torn, that gong-tormented sea.

Ostensibly, chaos is broken by the taming power of art; but the governing power of the verb "break," as Helen Vendler has observed, "is spent long before the end of the stanza is reached, and the last three lines stand syntactically as absolutes." In short, the literally overwhelming climactic sentence pours back into the poem all the turbulent, spawning images—and all the human torment—its marmoreal scenario had ostensibly left behind.

In these examples, Keats and Yeats, for all their ritualistic distancing and impersonalizing of pain, never lose sight of the reality of human suffering. Graves does—even though "To Juan at the Winter Solstice" is addressed to his own son. To clarify the difference, we might cite the nineteenth century's three chief theoreticians of the tragic. In Keats and Yeats, one senses the vision of Kierkegaard, with his emphasis upon the particular individual, rising up to counter that of Hegel, for whom the private grief of the sacrificial victim is absorbed into the all-reconciling universal order. In "To Juan," Graves is the most Hegelian of the three poets. But perhaps all might be brought together under the aegis of Nietzsche, who, while fully aware of the irreplaceability of individuals, wistfully longs to circumscribe suffering within a fuller glory—a "higher, overmastering joy" and order so transforming terror that "lamentation itself becomes a song of praise" (*The Birth of Tragedy*).

Lamentation becomes a song of praise, though not without an admixture of uncertainty, in another mythological love poem, "Darien." The poem begins in the present tense:

> It is a poet's privilege and fate
> To fall enamoured of the one Muse
> Who variously haunts this island earth.

The next line shifts tenses and reveals the poem to be, like "To Juan," a quasi-dramatic monologue: "She was your mother, Darien." The direct address of father to son is surprising here given the burden of what follows: the sacrificial death of the father in order to bring his (and her) son into the world. Before encountering that paradox, however, let us have Graves's elaborate description of the Muse Goddess:

> She was your mother, Darien,
> And presaged by the darting halcyon bird
> Would run green-sleeved along her ridges,
> Treading the asphodels and heather-trees
> With white feet bare.
>
> Often at sunrise I had watched her go,
> And a cold shudder shook me
> To see the curved blaze of her Cretan axe.
> Averted her set face, her business
> Not yet with me, long-striding,
> She would ascend the peak and pass from sight.
> But once at full moon, by the sea's verge,
> I came upon her without warning.
>
> Unrayed she stood, with long hair streaming,
> A cockle-shell cupped in her warm hands,
> Her axe propped idly on a stone.
>
> No awe possessed me, only a great grief;
> Wanly she smiled, but would not lift her eyes
> (As a young girl will greet the stranger).

His reaction is ambivalent. Does his grief reflect hers, that of a shy young girl deterministically trapped (like Coleridge's Geraldine or one of Hardy's "Subalterns") in her cruel, archetypal role? Or was he grieved essentially because he realized his time was at hand? Or because she had not yet marked him for her own? She too was uncertain. When he spoke to her (" 'See who has come,' I said"), she answered: " 'If I lift my eyes to yours / And our eyes marry, man, what then? / Will they engender my son Darien?' " She shares the procreant urge of Yeats's swan-god, but the issue, though named, remains occult, the sense of concealed mystery extending to her final description of that son as "Guardian of the *hid* treasures of the world."

One thing, however, is certain. Observing the anticipatory trembling of the Goddess's hands, the man recognized, and accepted, his fate: I knew then . . . / For whom that flawless blade would sweep: / My own oracular head, swung by its hair." He had no need then to ask for whom the bell tolled. But as her chosen man, he became the Goddess's prophet as well as her victim. " 'Mistress,' I cried, 'the times are evil / And you have charged me with their remedy.' "[71] In this spirit of apocalyptic Romanticism, he pleads only that she "look up, so Darien may be born!"

That request would seem to seal his fate. But the unmistakable implication of the imagery he employs in describing the prophesied son as "deathless," the "topless branch" of the Muse's "unfellable tree," and (climactically) "The new green of my hope" is that in embracing death he is really choosing a new, and rejuvenated, life; praying that, all autumnal foliage gone, he may shoot into a newly greened, vernal joy. That resurrection beyond martyrdom is implicit in the ecstatic final plea, an exclamation both doom-eager and hungry for renewal: " 'Sweetheart,' said I, 'strike now, for Darien's sake!' "

That the poet-lover should be more than half in love with death, that he has such celerity in dying, can be explained only if, reborn phoenixlike from his own sacrifice, he is able to continue singing after his decapitation by the Goddess. This extends the conclusion of "End of Play," where "We stare at our dazed trunks at the block kneeling," and looks forward to Orpheus's question in the later poem "Eurydice": "Is ours a fate can ever be forsworn / Though my lopped head sing to the yet unborn?" The "oracular head" of "Darien" is clearly to be connected with the prophetic head of Orpheus, which recalls for Graves as well the singing head of the decapitated Welsh god Bran (*The Greek Myths* 1:113–14). And all of this bizarre material links up with the ritual sacrifices of mortal man to immortal queen in Yeats's late dance-plays, *The King of the Great Clock Tower* and its revised version, *A Full Moon in March*, in which severed heads also sing on in an oracular strain.

If there is an element here of sadomasochistic savagery parading as mythology, Yeats seems more guilty than Graves. In "Darien," the mythological paradigm supports the poetic theme. Just as the old king, surrogate of the departing year, must be slain to make way for the new, so the middle-aged poet (wrinkled, but, like Darien, "grey-eyed")[72] must willingly yield up his old self in order to create the vital new poetry inherent in his visionary marriage with the Muse—a promise embodied in the living form of their son. Graves's parable is part of that genre so typical of Romantic and post-Romantic poetry: works about the relationship between the poet and his poem, the sacrifice he makes in order to create. As in Hart Crane's "The Broken Tower," it is the poet's self-sacrifice that liberates his music.

"Only look up, so Darien may be born!" When poet and Muse look at each other it can only be with what Keats calls, in his sonnet of eagle-eyed discovery and wonder, "a wild surmise." For whatever the certitude resident in the deterministic theme, mystery persists at the heart of the actual poem: "What then? / Will [our joined eyes] engender my son Darien?" Though the answer is apparently Yes, this embedded caveat, this element of uncertainty, adds at least some dramatic tension to the narrative. One thing about which there can be little or no doubt is that Keats's poem, the last word of which is "Darien," stands behind Graves's. The new planet that swims into the speaker's ken is Darien himself, the star-son of the Goddess: "the northern star, the spell of knowledge," as his father-to-be calls him in breathless anticipation.[73]

The Goddess's own description of Darien as "Swifter than wind, . . . Untameable," links the poem as well with Shelley's "Ode to the West Wind." That wind, a pestilence-cleansing harbinger of the apocalyptic spring to come, is, like its prophet, "tameless, and swift, and proud," though he is admittedly "less free / Than thou, O uncontrollable." Like Shelley, Graves, his own leaves falling and in sore need, is invoking, *incorporating*, a renovating power capable of driving his dead thoughts over the universe "Like withered leaves to quicken a new birth!" As Graves has put it in prose, "the pre-Celtic White Goddess was Death, but she granted peotic immortality to the victim whom she had seduced by her love-charms. . . . For though she loves only to destroy, the Goddess destroys only to quicken" (*WG*, pp. 432, 434). The purpose of that destruction of "whatever is overblown, faded, and dull" is "to clear the way for a new sowing" (*WG*, p. 446). The Gravesian speaker in this poem, in effect, says to Darien, "Be thou me." That swift, untameable child will be at once the speaker's re-created self and the apocalyptic "remedy" in an evil time; in both cases, he is "The new green of my hope." For if winter comes, can spring be far behind?

In "The White Goddess," originally published as the dedicatory poem to the volume of that title, the promise of fecund spring sustains the true quester in bleakest winter. The seeker (singular in the dedicatory poem, a plural "we" in *Poems and Satires 1951* and in *Collected Poems*) acts in defiance of the conventional world: the saints and sober men who, "Ruled by the God Apollo's golden mean," revile the Goddess. In predictable "scorn" of the life- and imagination-denying Apollonians,

> we sailed to find her
> In distant regions likeliest to hold her
> Whom we desired above all things to know,
> Sister of the mirage and echo.

Though she seems hopelessly remote and tenuous in the extreme, there *is* the fascination of what's difficult. The sea expedition is undertaken with infectious confidence, a confidence rewarded with the imaginative fleshing out of the mirage:

> It was a virtue not to stay,
> To go our headstrong and heroic way
> Seeking her out at the volcano's head,
> Among pack ice, or where the track had faded
> Beyond the cavern of the seven sleepers:
> Whose broad high brow was white as any leper's,
> Whose eyes were blue, with rowan-berry lips,
> With hair curled honey-coloured to white hips.

Though full appreciation of her sensuous beauty is troubled and confused by the traditional (*WG*, p. 431ff.) and Coleridgean leper comparison, the rich alliteration and assonance of the final lines sweep most doubt away. These lines, and the final stanza as a whole, reveal, as Kirkham says (p. 207), a "romanticism more full-bodied" than that of any previous Graves poem:

Green sap of Spring in the young wood a-stir
Will celebrate the Mountain Mother,
And every song-bird shout awhile for her;
But we are gifted, even in November
Rawest of seasons, with so huge a sense
Of her nakedly worn magnificence
We forget cruelty and past betrayal,
Heedless of where the next bright bolt may fall.

The Gravesian incantation is as magnificent as his God-dess, whose nakedness is that of the whole truth and nothing but the truth. "Truth has been represented by poets as a naked woman: a woman divested of all garments or orna-ments that will commit her to any particular position in time and space. The Syrian Moon-goddess was . . . represented so, with a snake head-dress to remind the devotee that she was Death in disguise" (*WG*, p. 448). This poem's romanti-cism is as "full-bodied" as it is precisely because it incorpo-rates the full paradox of death in disguise: the truth that beyond the longed-for spring we glimpse in raw winter there still lurks the "curved blaze" of her Cretan ax—here, the "bright bolt" that, balancing the green sap that rises in the spring, shall fall *in* the fall. For in ivy time, just as the flowers shall once again be trampled down by the great boar, the quester must die at the hands of she whom he desired above all things to "know." Indeed, emphasis is placed on knowl-edge. The birds and flowers celebrate her in season; "we," who have struggled through hardship to find her and are alone conscious of what is to come, hail the Goddess prolep-tically, with expectancy of both her generosity and her ulti-mate destructive blow.

Instead of masochism, however, there is a wonderful recklessness in the final alleged suspension of memory. Though in fact the lines look before and after, the acknowl-edged "cruelty and past betrayal" are, if not quite forgotten, absorbed; "we" are caught up in the spirit of headstrong and heroic *sprezzatura*, "Heedless of where the next bright bolt may fall." This is the "wasteful virtue," the nonchalant ges-ture in the face of danger and death, that so enraptured Yeats when he encountered it in that strong enchanter, Nietzsche.

Here it is caught perfectly by Graves, who finds—in sound and majestic cadence—the bravura adequate to his great theme.

VI

The White Goddess poems seem "major." And, indeed, Graves has done almost all those things major poets do. He has written a great deal of poetry and, through revision and winnowing (judicious until recent years), has established a canon. An occasionalist in many modes and tones, he eventually sought a central, focusing theme. He found it, for both his mythological studies and his practice of poetry, in love. Love is the main theme and origin of true poems, he believes, and the true poet writes *with* love, treating poetry with a single-minded "devotion" that may be called "religious." Graves's religion is his myth of the White Goddess and, since 1959, her Black sister. The neolithic and Bronze Age religious faith in the Triple Goddess has survived among what are called the Romantic poets, and Graves is convinced that his studies have shown that the imagery of the authentic Romantics was drawn, either consciously or unconsciously, from the cult of the Goddess and that the "magic" their poems exert largely depends on an intimacy with her mysteries (*OP*, pp. 230–31).

What for Graves is a central theme will seem to others merely eccentric; what to him is the persistent survival of a timeless motif is for others an atavistic aberration. And yet, despite his obsession with the ancient world—with love magic and poetic magic, with dragons and dreams and rites of blood, with ancient Welsh prosody, Sufi mysticism, and Celtic romance—Graves is a man of the modern world. He fought in that war which has itself come to seem a zigzag trench cutting through this century, dividing the old from the "modern" consciousness; and he has lived long enough to see both his island retreat and his most esoteric speculations domesticated by cultural tourists. He may find little to admire in the modern world, but he is certainly aware of what it is he spits from his mouth.

There is, then, a considerable body of work—much, though by no means all, of it now conveniently available in *New Collected Poems*. There is a central theme: that "one story and one story only / That will prove worth your telling." There is an elaborate mythography and a vital poetic tradition to buttress the theme, to provide a larger sustaining context for the hundreds of skillfully crafted lyrics that make up Graves's poetic corpus. And there is Graves himself: soldier, scholar, craftsman he; a figure larger than life, yet a man whose sophisticated primitivism, whose characteristically modern double-mindedness, makes him our contemporary.

But Graves remains an anomaly. We seldom think of him as a "major" poet, certainly not as a major *modern* poet. A case can be made (and has, by Kirkham) for his modernity on the basis of sensibility and awareness rather than of themes, images, and advanced techniques; and certainly the author of *Good-Bye to All That* is aware of twentieth-century chaos and brutality and of the modern patriarchy and mechanarchy he repudiates. He also repudiates "Franco-American modernism" with its "major poems of truly contemporary malaise" written for "an aggregate public." While he denies opposing innovations in poetic technique, he is clearly wary of them and of the often extreme explorations of sensibility we associate with Eliot, Pound, and the later Yeats. The problems of sensibility and awareness in Graves have to do, not with his experience of the modern world, but with his failure to consistently translate that experience into poetry.

There is something at once heroic and perverse in Graves's stance. Yeats, a poetic traditionalist too, felt himself to be a man "flung upon this filthy modern tide" ("The Statues"); but he entered, however quirkily, the waters of poetic modernism and so was reborn after midlife. Graves has never ceased regarding the "foul tidal basin of modernism" (*OP*, p. 281) as a stagnant deviation from the mainstream of tradition. For him, the genuine poet, independent of fashion and of public service, is a servant only of the true Muse, committed on her behalf to "continuous personal variations on a single prehistoric, or post-historic, poetic theme." Writing in 1949 (in the introduction to *The Common Asphodel*), and by then persuaded that he was himself such a Muse-poet, he tells us, in a most revealing metaphor, that he has "ceased to feel the frantic strain of swimming against the stream of time."

Actually, Graves had largely reconciled himself to swimming in his own way, against the modern mainstream, by the early thirties. And, with characteristic pride and cunning, he had turned his "limitations" into a claimed advantage. "Flying Crooked" is perhaps the best of his anecdotes on the theme, a poem in which he chooses an image emblematic for Yeats as well: the butterfly. The older poet, who associated "zigzag wantonness" and the "crooked road of intuition" with the eccentric flight of that insect, wore a ring depicting butterfly and hawk and liked to autograph books with the explanatory lines: "wisdom is a butterfly / And not a gloomy bird of prey." At the same time, of course, Yeats was attracted to straight-flying predatory birds of war and chose as his central hero Cuchulain, that "clean hawk out of the air." In "Rocky Acres," Graves too identified with the unburgherly predator who, hovering in the air, rocking on his wings, "scans his wide parish with a sharp eye." But in more whimsical, and more persuasive, moods he adopts as his own the zigzag crooked path:

> The butterfly, a cabbage-white,
> (His honest idiocy of flight)
> Will never now, it is too late,
> Master the art of flying straight,
> Yet has—who knows so well as I?—
> A just sense of how not to fly:
> He lurches here and here by guess
> And God and hope and hopelessness.
> Even the aerobatic swift
> Has not his flying-crooked gift.

Behind the precision of observation (even the species is identified) the parallel with Graves's own idiosyncratic strategy as a poet ("who knows so well as I?") is obvious.[74] If

Graves's flight is eccentric, even "idiotic," it is also—and, here again, we must read in the contrast with the other modern idols, especially Yeats—"honest." And whatever he lacks to qualify as a "master" of the "art of flying straight" he makes up for in the possession of good sense and a mysterious "gift" in comparison with which that dubious mastery seems well lost. It is a variation on a recurrent paradox in Graves's "interaction" with his contemporaries: his recognition not merely that it is "too late" to teach an old aeronaut like himself the new tricks of the hawks, the alleged masters of mainstream modernist poetry, but also that his "flying-crooked gift" is actually superior to their "straight" but, by implication, *dis*honest (and therefore *morally* "crooked") aerobatic skills.

In "Flying Crooked," Graves typically celebrates his chosen crookedness in a craftsmanlike way—here, in impeccably metrical couplets (iambic tetrameters rather than pentameters; that they were the choice of Jonathan Swift in the age of the heroic couplet opens the possibility of a pun in Graves's penultimate line). As usual, too, the Romantic-intuitive is in balance with the Classical-rational aspect of double-minded Graves. Like the butterfly (and like the bat in Richard Wilbur's poem "Mind"), Graves "lurches" about "by guess" yet has a "just sense" of how *not* to fly, of what to avoid. And though, like other honest idiots, he is a child of "God," he seems directed less by that male divinity than by the "hope and hopelessness" associated with a Muse Goddess who, however deterministic, is no less wanton and wayward than the flight of a butterfly and whose power will eventually be epitomized in the crooked (*cur-vus*), "curved blaze of her Cretan axe" ("Darien").

In a thematically related poem of the same period, "In Broken Images," Graves contrasts the quick, confident, linear rationalist who thinks in clear images with himself, "slow, thinking in broken images." But in mistrusting his images and questioning their relevance, he becomes "sharp" as the clear-thinker grows "dull." And whereas when "fact fails" the logician he can only "question" his physical senses and instincts, Graves can "approve" his. So both continue, "He in a new confusion of his understanding; / I in a new understanding of my confusion." No images, clear or broken, appear in the poem. Yet even so abstract an exercise in verbal gymnastics demonstrates Graves's skill, the poem's construction (propositions in couplets) parodying as it does the discourse of Apollonian logicians. It also demonstrates, and exemplifies, Graves's ability to turn acknowledged limitations into an occasion for triumph: another instance of Goliath being toppled by underdog, "minor" David.

One way to pull off such triumphs is to claim to be part of the "true" mainstream. If modernist poetry was bogus, complex, ambiguous, stylistically idiosyncratic, dislocated, and pretentiously "major," then true poetry, consisting of personal variations on a single timeless theme, must be lucid, ecstatic, traditionalist, and—deliberately, aggressively— "minor." Graves, who has been called "the most prideful poet writing in the world today," has dismissed not only Auden and Thomas, but Yeats, Eliot, Pound, and Wallace Stevens as well: it has been observed that "if it is true Graves won't suffer fools gladly, it is even truer he suffers his betters not at all."[75] At the same time, he himself eschews all claim to being a major poet. "Minor poetry, so called to differentiate it from major poetry, is the real stuff," he insists, pride characteristically mingling with that sense of limitation (*OP*, p. 261).

At this point, critics tend to become either consciously playful or annoyed with the distinction as an extrinsic or wrongfully applied standard. George Stade opens his monograph on Graves by declaring him "a minor poet of major proportions"; David Bromwich, concluding his brief review of *New Collected Poems*, asks, "Is Graves a minor poet? A major poet? A major minor poet? A minor major poet?" and concludes by understandably passing the buck: "There are those who will enjoy deciding."[76] The real enjoyment, of course, comes in reading the best of Graves's poetry. In his full-scale study, Kirkham avoids throughout the classification of Graves's work as either major or minor on the ground that these are "vague categories usually implying standards extrinsic to literary judgment" (p. 274). Thom Gunn, a poet influenced by Graves, has suggested that professional critics, confronted with Graves's versatility, have taken refuge in the formula that, though he is admittedly accomplished, he is minor. Somebody's standards are wrong, Gunn concludes, and that somebody isn't Graves (*Shenandoah* symposium, pp. 34–35).

Graves himself treats the distinction as critical shoptalk and, more significantly, as an Apollonian conspiracy against the Muse and her poets. In his essay "Sweeney among the Blackbirds," he declares all "magic poems" to be the work of young people. But the poet, as he grows "old and reasonable," tends to lose his power of falling in love, or even of remaining in love.

> The Literary Establishment has a bright label for what he then produces, if he follows the right models energetically enough. It is "Major Poetry"—which casually consigns the magical poems of his early manhood to the category "Minor Poems." Having by this time graduated as a solid member of society, the new major poet transfers his allegiance from the White Goddess of Inspiration to Apollo, the god of musical and artistic achievement—the all-too-reasonable upstart godling who dethroned the great Ninefold Muse-goddess of Greece, reduced her to nine little obedient Muses. (*OP*, pp. 256–57)

The transfer of allegiance from the White Goddess to Apollo, from ecstatic Muse poetry to nonecstatic, architectural, "major" Apollonian poetry, is the Gravesian sin against the spirit. "Nothing," he has said in a lecture on the legitimate criticism of poetry, "is better than the truly good, not even the truly great. . . . Good poets are exceedingly rare; 'great poets' are all too common. The poet who accepts his limitations but works to the point of exhaustion on getting every word of a poem into place, may yet fail, for one reason or another, to be as good as he intends" (*OP*, pp. 221, 225). Nevertheless, such an honest worker shall

> mount and keep his distant way
> Beyond the limits of a vulgar fate:
> Beneath the Good how far—but far above the Great.

Even if we grant (I do) the partial validity of Graves's

95

distinction, we yet pull up short of full assent—both to the general proposition and to its application to Graves himself: an idiosyncratic but perhaps major mythographer and a dedicated craftsman who, to alter his own distinction, stands firmly among the Good, but *beneath* the Great how far.

The Great I have had in mind throughout much of the present study are the Great Romantics, Graves's precursors both in devotion to the Muse and as mythmakers. While there is truth in Harold Bloom's observation that, unlike the "First Romantics," the "Last Romantics" (Yeats, Lawrence, and Graves) have succumbed to "shamanism" and "phantasmagoria," with the darkest phantasmagoria Graves's masochistic insistence on "the mutual rendings of poet and Muse as being true love,"[77] it is equally true that Gravesian wildness is tempered by stoicism and a stress on limitation. For Graves, true poetry is by definition minor poetry. The chief popular impact of the Great Romantics, too, has been achieved with short lyrics rather than with their attempted or accomplished epics. But even if those precursor-poems for Graves—"The Mental Traveller," "The Ancient Mariner," and the most condensed of these epical ballads, "La Belle Dame sans Merci"—were to be considered minor, the fact remains that the ambition of Blake, Coleridge, and Keats (one shared by Wordsworth and Shelley) was to create major poetry, specifically to out-Milton Milton. In contrast to these titanic overreachers and failed questers, Graves is teleological. His reach seldom if ever exceeds his grasp. Though surprise was a notable element in his earlier poems, the later ones seem sometimes so predictable that their end is in their beginning. And his vision, for all his abandonment to the vagaries of the Goddess, remains stoic rather than apocalyptic.

I am not arguing with Graves's dualistic temperament, a double-mindedness that has provided one of my main themes. But if we are reminded of Hardy and Frost, stoic traditional poets whom Graves admires, we must also remember not only that they are "major" poets compared to him, but also that they share little of his mythopoeic extravagance, his phantasmagoria. And yet, for all his attunement to archetypal mysteries, Graves is even more obsessed than they with the minutiae of craftsmanship and the need for poems to make "good sense." It is not necessary to endorse shoddy craftsmanship or perverse obscurity to observe the inherent dangers in such a program as Graves's. As he himself admitted in a preface to a reading, some of his later poems are so "cunning" that they lack exuberance (*Steps*, p. 236).

To adapt T. E. Hulme's celebrated distinction between the Romantic and the Classic, Graves seems a poet who, while fully conscious of the vast ocean around him, prefers to dip his bucket in a limited well. And this Romantic-Classic distinction may be applied to that between major and minor poetry. In one unreprinted poem that clarifies the poet-Muse relationship, the ephebe is advised:

> Never sing a song clean through,
>   You might disenchant her,
> Venture on a verse or two
> (Indisposed to sing it through),
> Let that seem as much as you
>   Care, or dare, to grant her.[78]

The jaunty rhythms of light verse embody the problem. For it seems less a fear of the Muse that inhibits Graves than his own sense of limitation and the precariousness of that bond with her that provides enchanted inspiration. One "dare" not press too far: to be disposed to "sing a song clean through" is to be willing both to penetrate to the experiential sources of creativity and to take the ambitious risks that separate major poetry from a modest verse or two. "Indisposed," "seem," and "care" slyly suggest that the effort is actually being made under a defensive show of laconic wit and nonchalance. But in fact Graves is rarely willing to "venture" into either length of conceptual depth. It may be true, as he says, that "all Muse poetry is minor poetry, if length be the criterion" (*OP*, p. 299), but it seems suspiciously convenient that his Muse should prefer brief finger exercises to ambitious odes.

This is an uncharitable way to put it, and unfair to Graves, who has after all produced an impressive and well-wrought body of work. His poetry—characterized by a lucid, tempered awe in face of the phantasmagoria he himself evokes—is poetry of the British middle ground, its climate of thought generally located in the temperate zone, content to be native and traditional in both technique and theme. *"Vers libre* could come to nothing in England," Thomas Hardy assured an admiring Graves in the twenties. "All we can do is to write on the old themes in the old styles, but try to do it a little better than those who went before us" (*Good-Bye to All That*, p. 307). Graves has from the beginning maintained a traditionalist belief that certain principles cannot be violated without poetry turning into something else, and though his distillation of Hardy's "old themes" into the "one story" of his monomyth may seem idiosyncratic, that theme is, in Graves's eyes, even more traditional than his conservative poetic technique.

And he is proud of his old-fashioned virtues. An American critic recently complained in the *New York Times Book Review*: "Robert Graves, the British veteran, is no longer in the poetic swim. He still resorts to traditional metres and rhyme, and to such out-dated words as *tilth*; withholding his 100% approbation also from contemporary poems that favor sexual freedom." It is hard not to be won over by the veteran's response:

> Gone are the drab monosyllabic days
> When "agricultural labour" still was *tilth*;
> And "100% approbation," *praise*;
> And "pornographic modernism," filth—
> Yet still I stand by *tilth* and *filth* and *praise*.

Here as elsewhere, craft triumphs over crankiness. This little poem, which might have been no more than a bit of reactionary grumbling, is manipulated so that the last line not only scoops up the three operative terms but concludes resonantly, its final word, "praise," elevating the poem well above its germinal anger. Reading "Tilth," one feels no inclination to take issue with an arrogance that on other occasions can be monstrous. The stubbornness of "Yet still I stand" here seems admirable. Like Swift and Yeats, Graves feels himself a man appointed to guard a position. "Stand we on guard oath-bound," Yeats defiantly asserted in his deathbed poem "The Black Tower"; those banners of materialistic modernism "come not in."

Graves's stubborn "stand" is also the final position of an old man ("Tilth" was written in the seventies). At the end of the story as at its beginning, Graves's soldierly stance is both perverse and heroic, poignant and admirable. "The pride of 'bearing it out even to the edge of doom' that sustains a soldier in the field," he has written in a characteristic fusion of Shakespeare, war, and poetry, "governs a poet's service to the Muse."

> It is not masochism, or even stupidity, but a determinism that the story shall end gloriously: a willingness to risk all wounds and hardships, to die weapon in hand. For a poet this defiance is, of course, metaphorical: death means giving in to dead forces, dead routines of action and thought. The Muse represents eternal life and the sudden lightning-flash of wisdom. (*OP*, p. 539)

If pride, determination, length of dedicated service, and courage in the field were the only criteria, Robert Graves would be second to no poet of this century, not even to Yeats. But they are not the only criteria; and Graves, for all his indisputable achievement and valiant refusal to give in to dead forces, remains a poet whose story ends honorably rather than gloriously.

Above all, it ends, Graves insists, with poetic integrity and commitment to that truthfulness he denied in Yeats. Yet as Pindar, Nietzsche's Zarathustra, and Zarathustrian Yeats have acknowledged, a poet's very skill can make him a liar. Auden once called Graves's natural facility for writing verse a valuable but dangerous gift, for the poet who possesses it "can all too easily forsake the truth for verbal display" (*Shenandoah* symposium, p. 8). The source is as significant as the substance of the criticism. What has been said of Auden's employment of Skaldic meters and of the verbal tricks of late

Norse poetry (that it can produce a verse that, in Goethe's phrase, "does the poet's thinking for him," and so can become a "substitute for any deeper movement and expansion of the poet's mind") might be said of Graves's employment of Welsh and Anglo-classical prosodic "tricks," particularly his use of *cynghanedd* and allied techniques of alliteration, assonance, and internal rhyming.[79] There is, after all, no guarantee that an intricately "crafted" poem will not be trivial.

It was precisely this charge—technical skill concealing a nullity of thought and "truth"—that, as we've seen, Graves leveled against later Yeats, who had "a new technique, but nothing to say," and who, bereft of a true Muse, employed "a ventriloquist's dummy." Perhaps with that example in mind, Graves declared in the Oxford lectures that "technique takes one no farther than articulating the skeletons [in Ezekiel's valley of dry bones] with wire, and plumping them up with plastic limbs and organs," whereas when poetry is treated in the true spirit, "the notion of technique falls away"; all that remains is the acolyte's service to the Muse, "his unwavering love of whom, for all her unpossessibility, assures that his work will be truthful" (*OP*, p. 425). Will the preserved poems of the dedicated poet "figure as durable records of blessedness," or merely "convey, truthfully, the darkness of his self-deception?" That seems to double-minded Graves a philosophical, and therefore "irrelevant," question. "A poet's destiny is to love" (*OP*, pp. 595–96).

Despite the lesser, thinner work of recent years, much of which sacrifices passionate intensity to a love-"magic" and "togetherness" more tedious than serene, Graves is a craftsman rather than a mere technician. His poems may be said to succeed or fail insofar as they fulfill the implications of the marvelous concluding line of his most celebrated lyric: "But nothing promised that is not performed." Beyond the bittersweet fruit of the votary's pact with his Goddess— ecstasy shadowed by the inevitable ax—the line implies that the poet puts on *something* of the power and knowledge of the Muse: that nothing is numinously conceived that is not executed by the devotee as man and craftsman. Though there are exceptions (of which "To Juan at the Winter Solstice" is among the most obvious), Graves's most ambitious work falls short of its promise when it fails, in performance, to memorably and dramatically embody the myth. Even in poems with few if any mythopoeic pretensions, failure results when Graves is too rationally reined in or when he succumbs to abstraction. Too often he tells rather than shows—and despite his deserved reputation as a love poet, the later lyrics only sporadically make us feel the passion Graves asserts.

But then there are the poems in which Graves succeeds. There are many of these; and the qualities that make them admirable—clarity, flexibility of tone and diction, syntactical and verbal precision, ironic wit and a genuine balance between wildness and civility—ought to recommend them to a wider audience. This is especially true at a time when the "common reader" of poetry, who still hankers after sense and meaning, has virtually nowhere to turn; when poetry itself has dwindled to a province largely restricted to practitioners and academicians. In Graves's tradition—though he sometimes grandly announces that he writes poems only for poets—the poet is still a man speaking to others. Poets who "serve the Muse" must wait for the "inspired lightning flash of two or three words that initiate composition and dictate the rhythmic norm"—what later Graves calls *báraka*, an Islamic word meaning lightning, the "sudden divine rapture" that overcomes devotees. But the result, however "lightning-struck" its inception, must communicate. (*OP*, pp. 431, 359–60, 366) The doctrine and its imagery inform "Dance of Words" (1964), a poem that embodies the interaction of chance and discipline, puzzling magic and plain sense, individual rhythm and traditional form:

> To make them move, you should start from lightning
> And not forecast the rhythm: rely on chance,
> Or so-called chance for its bright emergence
> Once lightning interpenetrates the dance.

Grant them their own traditional steps and postures
But see they dance it out again and again
Until only lightning is left to puzzle over—
The choreography plain, and the theme plain.

In two loosely formal quatrains (alternating between feminine and masculine endings, rhyming on the even lines, prosodically a Gravesian variation on iambic), "Dance of Words" traces poetic genesis to the inexplicable mysteries of *báraka* but insists that the product of that private inspiration make good public sense, its form and content unembellished and comprehensible. The poem itself is another instance of that wild civility characteristic of double-minded Graves at his balanced best. He may not be a "major" poet, and he is certainly not in the modernist swim, but Robert Graves's accomplishment—reflected, at its best, in his ability to start from mystery and yet render the choreography plain and the theme plain—makes him too good a poet to be politely dismissed, and considerably more than an archaic torso washed up at Majorca and out of the swing of the sea.

NOTES

1. The poem, written in the late fifties, appears in *New Collected Poems* (New York: Doubleday, 1977) with *verses* (l. 4) misprinted as *verse*, one of the less forgivable carelessnesses in this carelessly produced volume. For Lysander's lines, see *A Midsummer Night's Dream*, 3. 2. 252–53 (Pelican edition). Steiner's comment is at the end of his "The Genius of Robert Graves" (for full information on this and other critical essays and books on Graves, see n. 11).

2. "The Age of Obsequiousness," in *On Poetry: Collected Talks and Essays* (New York: Doubleday, 1969), p. 43. Hereafter referred to as *OP*.

3. The poem originally appeared in *On English Poetry: Being an Irregular Approach to the Psychology of This Art, from Evidence Mainly Subjective* (New York: Knopf; London: Heinemann, 1922); then in *Poems 1914–1926* (London: Heinemann, 1927), and in *Collected Poems* (London: Cassell, 1938).

4. Limits of space and subject restrict my references to the voluminous prose of Graves, whose extra-poetic canon, cut to essentials, would include perhaps a dozen of his almost one hundred volumes. Of his translations, the least dispensable is *The Golden Ass* of Apuleius (1950, 1951); of his novels, the most compelling remain *I, Claudius* and its sequel (1934, 1935), and—less for the fiction than for the mythography—*The Golden Fleece* (1944; published in the United States in 1945 as *Hercules, My Shipmate*) and *King Jesus* (1946). Short fiction appears in *Occupation: Writer* (1950, 1951), *Collected Short Stories* (1964, 1965), and *The Shout and Other Stories* (1979). Much of Graves's poetic criticism has been conveniently gathered in two collections. *The Common Asphodel* (1949), covering 1922–1949, contains material from books published by Graves alone and in collaboration with Laura Riding, as well as essays (on Nietzsche and the Romantic poets) reprinted from *Epilogue*, their midthirties periodical. The other collection of talks and essays carries iconoclasm to often idiosyncratic extremes. *On Poetry* (1969) puts between two covers the calumnious Clark lectures (first printed in *The Crowning Privilege*, 1955), most of *5 Pens in Hand* and *Steps* (1958), and *Poetic Craft and Principle* (1967), which itself consisted of the *Oxford Addresses on Poetry* (1962), *Mammon and the Black Goddess* (1965), and an essay on the word *romantic*.

Three works in particular cannot be ignored. The first is *Good-bye to All That* (1929, 1957), the war memoir that established Graves's fame. Equally celebrated, if less consistently readable, is that dragon at the entrance to Graves's mythopoeic cave, *The White Goddess* (1948, later amended). Finally, the blend of erudition and intuitive audacity that understandably infuriates classical scholars is displayed in *The Greek Myths* (1955), a splendid retelling of the old stories buttressed by Gravesian glosses that are intriguing even when they are most dubious.

5. *New York Times Magazine*, 1 April 1979, p. 53.

6. William David Thomas has been exploring Graves's textual var-

iants, a study of which he hopes will lead eventually to a complete variorum edition of the poems.

7. See Graves's Oxford thesis, published as *Poetic Unreason and Other Studies* (London: Cecil Palmer, 1925).

8. Though Graves praises Horatian elegance, balance, and "skilful gleemanship," Horace is not among his "true" poets. And while George Steiner is right to place Graves's lyrics in "that small corner of English literature which is genuinely Latin" (*The Death of Tragedy* [New York: Knopf, 1961], p. 30), even Graves's favorite poet in the Graeco-Roman tradition—the original, fearless, and sincerely woman-loving Catullus—is described as transcending that tradition; "the reason perhaps was that he was of Celtic birth" (*WG*, p. 392).

9. Ransom, in the third *Fugitive* (October 1922); Shapiro, in the penultimate chapter of *In Defense of Ignorance* (1960).

10. "Does America Have a Major Poet?" *New York Times Book Review*, 3 December 1978, p. 9.

11. Fraser's "The Poetry of Robert Graves," which first appeared in 1947, was reprinted in 1959 and, with two brief afterthoughts, in 1977 in his *Essays on Twentieth Century Poets* (Leicester: Leicester University Press, 1977). Randall Jarrell's two-part article "Graves and the White Goddess," which appeared first in *Yale Review* 45 (Winter, Spring, 1956), is reprinted in Jarrell's *The Third Book of Criticism* (New York: Farrar, Straus and Giroux, 1966). Martin Seymour-Smith, *Robert Graves* (London: Longmans, Green for the British Council, 1956). J. M. Cohen, *Robert Graves* (Edinburgh: Oliver and Boyd, 1960; New York: Evergreen, 1961). George Steiner, "The Genius of Robert Graves," *Kenyon Review* 22 (Summer 1960): 340–65. Ronald Gaskell, "The Poetry of Robert Graves," *The Critical Quarterly* 3(Autumn 1961): 213–22. Douglas Day, *Swifter than Reason: The Poetry and Criticism of Robert Graves* (Chapel Hill: The University of North Carolina Press, 1963). Michael Kirkham, *The Poetry of Robert Graves* (New York: Oxford University Press, 1969). Daniel Hoffman, *Barbarous Knowledge: Myth in the Poetry of Yeats, Graves, and Muir* (New York: Oxford University Press, 1967). In addition, there have been two symposia devoted to Graves: in *Shenandoah* 13 (Winter 1962) and in *Malahat Review* 35 (July 1975); a penetrating review article, Monroe K. Spears, "The Latest Graves: Poet and Private Eye," *Sewanee Review* 73 (Autumn 1965): 660–78; another pamphlet, George Stade, *Robert Graves* (New York: Columbia University Press, 1967); two studies focusing on Graves as mythmaker: John B. Vickery, *Robert Graves and the White Goddess* (Lincoln: University of Nebraska Press, 1972) and James S. Mehoke, *Robert Graves: Peace-Weaver* (The Hague: Mouton, 1975); and a French study, Jean-Paul Forster, *Robert Graves et la dualité du réel* (Berne: Herbert Lang; Francfort/M: Peter Lang, 1975).

12. Harry Strickhausen, in *Poetry* 104 (July 1964).

13. *The White Goddess*, "Amended and Enlarged Edition" (New York: Farrar, Straus and Giroux, 1966), p. 486. Hereafter referred to as *WG*.

14. Shakespeare's future Henry V refers to cannon-shaped leather

sacks as "bombards" (*1 Henry IV*, 2. 4. 429), which may have suggested testicles in Graves's already Shakespearean poem. And of course there are many "breaching" images that are explicitly sexual in Shakespeare. Graves's second stanza—indeed, his whole priapic poem—probably echoes Henry V's "phallic" exhortation: "Once more into the breach," in which his soldiers are to "Stiffen the sinews, summon up the blood, / Disguise fair nature with hard-favored rage; / . . . / Hold hard the breath and bend up every spirit / To his full height!" (*Henry V*, 3. 1. 1–11).

15. *Caricature* is, incidentally, a crucial word—indeed, a leitmotiv—in Graves's *Good-bye to All That* (New York: Doubleday, 1957 [1929]); see pp. 180, 251, 272, 296, 307, 341.

16. *OP*, p. 34. It seems relevant to this poem, with its image of "retching" wind, that Graves's example of a disgusting trope is one of Cowley's on the wind.

17. Foreword to *Collected Poems 1955* (New York: Doubleday, 1955), p. xi.

18. Preface to *Whipperginny* (London: Heinemann; New York: Knopf, 1923). Foreword to the 1938 *Collected Poems*, p. xiii.

19. Graves, "Coleridge and Wordsworth," in *The Common Asphodel: Collected Essays on Poetry, 1922–1949* (London: Hamilton, 1949), pp. 235–45 (243).

20. *The Complete Poetical Works of Samuel Taylor Coleridge*, ed. E. H. Coleridge, 2 vols. (Oxford: Clarendon Press, 1912), 2:1111. Coincidentally, two of Coleridge's lines in the first draft of "Work Without Hope"—"at fancy's touch / Thought becomes image and I see it such"—anticipate Donald Davie's comment (in the *Shenandoah* symposium, p. 40) on the emblematic quality of Graves's poem: "Who can doubt that the rustic image of 'Love Without Hope' was specifically constructed . . . to stand as full and explicit counterpart to the abstractions of its title."

21. Rosemary Dinnage, "Dodgson's Passion" [a review of *The Letters of Lewis Carroll*], *New York Review of Books* 26 (16 August 1979): 13.

22. The poem was first published in *Ten Poems More* (Paris: Hours Press, 1930), and repeated, with the original three stanzas, in *Poems 1926–1930* (London: Heinemann, 1931).

23. "The Second-Fated." Graves's reported death, described in *Good-bye to All That*, is also the subject of the early poem "Escape."

24. This was its title in *Welchman's Hose* (London: The Fleuron, 1925). Graves and Riding quote Yeats's poem in the "Modernist Poetry and Civilization" chapter of *A Survey of Modernist Poetry*, written in 1926 and published in London by Heinemann in 1927. Since they could not have read the poem in *The Tower* (1928), they must have known it from its periodical publication (in *The Dial* and *The London Mercury* in 1921) or from its appearance in *Seven Poems and a Fragment* (Cuala Press, 1922). See below, p. 35.

25. "Cuirassiers" is a satire on corrupt civilians safe at home (cutthroats, "pederastic senators," and the eunuchs of the "draped saloons" of the metropolis) and on that other corruption, Christianity. The poem seems an

unqualified affirmation of the regimental pride that Graves (both in this poem and in his prose on the war) designates a "sacrament." But then comes the kind of final "surprise" Graves and Riding once compared to the "shock of a broken electric circuit." The wonderful last line—"A rotten tree lives only in its rind"—goes beyond the simple contrast of decadence and vitality to raise a question: If the sick Roman civilization is being supported only by the solid virtues and barbarian virility of its frontier guards, are they not part of the corruption? After all, that which is falling, says Nietzsche's Zarathustra, one should also push—not prolong.

26. *A Survey of Modernist Poetry* (Folcroft Library Edition, 1971 [1927]), pp. 176, 178. When this last passage was reprinted in 1949, Graves replaced "the old romantic weaknesses" with "confirmed literary habits" (*The Common Asphodel*, p. 136). Fuller's first name, given incorrectly in both texts, was Loie, not Lois.

27. "The Ghost of Milton" (1947), in *The Common Asphodel*, p. 322n.

28. *A Pamphlet Against Anthologies* (London: Cape, 1928), pp. 68, 95–102. *Innisfree* is misspelled *Inisfree* throughout the *Pamphlet*. The epigram, another small instance of interaction, is based on the ballad "Victim of a Squire's Whims."

29. "These Be Your Gods, O Israel!" (*OP*, p. 129).

30. The lecture, first printed in *Essays in Criticism* (April 1955), was responded to by Delmore Schwartz and Karl Shapiro when it appeared in *New Republic* in February and March 1956: Schwartz, 19 March; Shapiro, 2 April. I cite the lecture throughout from *OP* (pp. 127–52), unless otherwise indicated, from pp. 130–36.

31. Georgie Yeats had, of course, discovered an aptitude for automatic writing in 1917. Yeats is surely in Graves's mind in the final paragraph of chapter 24 of *The White Goddess*. After discussing various aids to inspiration, Graves observes that nowadays, "a good many of the charlatans or weaklings resort to automatic writing and spiritism" (*WG*, p. 441).

32. See *Ah, Sweet Dancer: W. B. Yeats, Margot Ruddock, a Correspondence*, ed. Roger McHugh (New York: Macmillan, 1970).

33. *Letters to W. B. Yeats*, ed. Richard J. Finneran, George Mills Harper, and William M. Murphy, 2 vols. (New York: Columbia University Press, 1977), 2:579–80. In a letter written one year later (23 April 1936), Laura Riding was gracious enough to say, "We should both be pleased to receive you" (2:610); but no meeting took place.

34. Dorothy Wellesley, *Letters on Poetry from W. B. Yeats to Dorothy Wellesley* (London: Oxford University Press, 1940), p. 64. Yeats's polite but "despotic" reply, quoted in the next paragraph, is cited from p. 67 of this volume.

35. The three letters that have survived from Laura Riding's correspondence with Yeats in the spring of 1936 have been printed as an appendix to *Letters to W. B. Yeats*, 2:609–11. The peripheral references to domestic despotism are an oblique response to Yeats's misconception that Graves and she were married, an error Laura Riding corrects repeatedly and, as she says,

"without humour" in all three letters.

36. Graves, "Nietzsche," an *Epilogue* essay reprinted in *The Common Asphodel*, p. 227. For the passage from *Thus Spake Zarathustra* and speculations on Nietzsche's noncognitivist doctrine of "necessary fictions," see my "On Truth and Lie in Nietzsche," *Salmagundi* 29 (Spring 1975): 67–94. Nietzsche was aware that the ancient Muses were notoriously untrustworthy and that even Pindar could admit, "Beauty, who creates All sweet delights for men, / Brings honor at will, and makes the false seem true / Time and again" (*Olympian*, 2. 30–34).

37. Nietzsche's famous remark (which appears in the *Viking Portable Nietzsche* as "Fragment on Schopenhauer") is echoed by Yeats in another letter to Moore: "Schopenhauer can do no wrong in my eyes; I no more quarrel with his errors than I do with a mountain cataract" (December 1927) in *W. B. Yeats and T. Sturge Moore: Their Correspondence*, ed. Ursula Bridge (London: Routledge & Kegan Paul, 1957).

38. *OP*, p. 128. The essay referred to, printed in the Spring 1937 number of *Epilogue*, was signed only with initials: L.R., R.G., and H.K. (Harry Kemp).

39. Graves does not identify the source of Mortimer's remarks; they are from his review of Richard Ellmann's *The Identity of Yeats*—"The Progress of a Poet," *Sunday Times* (London), 15 August 1954, p. 3. So annoyed is he in tracing the poet-alchemist analogy that while ridiculing Yeats's lack of chemical knowledge, Graves (as Colin Wilson once pointed out) slightly bungles his own chemistry.

40. It would be unfair to point out that not one reader in 10 million is likely to know who "Dame Ocupacyon" is. She is, in Skelton's "Garland of Laurell," the registrar or poetry critic employed by the Goddess of Fame—as Graves had told his immediate audience in the previous lecture in the series.

41. This fundamental misreading was first pointed out by Peter Ure, "Yeats and Mr. Graves," *Times Literary Supplement* 58 (12 June 1959): 353.

42. My formulation here paraphrases a remark of Richard Ellmann's on another Yeatsian persona, the Irish monk of *Supernatural Songs*; Ellmann has also anticipated me by noting the urbanity and slight irony of the woman in "Chosen." *The Identity of Yeats*, 2d ed. (New York: Oxford University Press, 1964), pp. 182, 167.

43. *OP*, p. 151. For the remarks on Eliot and Auden, see *OP*, pp. 141, 146. The despised Vergil also "never bore arms either for or against Caesar" ("The Anti-Poet," *OP*, p. 302).

44. *OP*, p. 131. The short poems Graves is alluding to, "A Coat" and "To a Poet, who would have me praise certain Bad Poets, Imitators of His and Mine," were written in 1914 and 1910 respectively.

45. This was the concluding statement of Yeats's final draft for a lecture delivered on 9 March 1910, but without this final flourish. See Joseph Ronsley, "Yeats's Lecture Notes for 'Friends of My Youth,' " in *Yeats and the Theatre*, ed. Robert O'Driscoll and Lorna Reynolds (Macmillan of Canada, 1975), pp. 61–81.

46. D. J. Enright, "The Example of Robert Graves," *Shenandoah* symposium, p. 14.

47. This revealingly chivalric-religious comment, made in conversation with Kathleen Nott, is reported in Seymour-Smith, *Robert Graves*, p. 16.

48. Patrick Grant, "The Dark Side of the Moon: Robert Graves as Mythographer," *Malahat Review* symposium, pp. 143–65 (155–56, 163).

49. Strictly speaking, Graves's first novel was one written with Laura Riding a year earlier: *No Decency Left* (1932), published under the pseudonym of "Barbara Rich."

50. In *Jesus in Rome*, we discover that Christ, having survived Calvary, is well and living in Italy.

51. I quote the succinct synopsis of Patrick Grant, who thinks the novel the most important book after *The White Goddess* "for understanding Graves' mythography." (*Malahat Review* symposium, p. 158).

52. *WG*, p. 486. The poem, untitled in *The White Goddess* and included in *Collected Poems 1914–1947*, was dropped in 1965. Perhaps it was too "Yeatsian."

53. *WG*, p. 458. This passage offers further evidence of Graves's double-mindedness. That women will turn Bassarids again en masse is at present "unlikely," though an "English or American woman in a nervous breakdown of sexual origin will often instinctively reproduce in faithful and disgusting detail much of the ancient Dionysiac ritual. I have witnessed it myself in helpless terror." Nietzsche, too, though he refused to dismiss Dionysian rites as mere cultural sicknesses, found in the sheer bestiality of pre-Hellenic Dionysian festivals "that abominable mixture of lasciviousness and cruelty which has always seemed to me the true 'witches' brew' " (*The Birth of Tragedy*, chap. 2).

54. Graves has a (pro-Trojan) poem on Hector's death at the hands of Achilles; and there too he echoes "The Tyger." See his translation of *The Iliad*, entitled *The Anger of Achilles* (1959), Book XXII.

55. With these Yeatsian poems of incubi and nightmares, cf. Graves's "The Succubus" and "Hag-Ridden."

56. *The Poetry of Robert Graves*, pp. 202–3. Kirkham is quoting from p. 17 of a book that Riding edited and for which she supplied a commentary. In the opening pages of *The Greek Myths* we are introduced to the primitive matriarch, whom men "feared, adored, and obeyed, ... the hearth which she tended in a cave or hut being their earliest social centre and motherhoood their prime mystery. Thus the first victim of a Greek sacrifice was always offered to Hestia of the Hearth" (1:11).

57. "The Genius of Robert Graves," p. 353.

58. *A Vision by W. B. Yeats: A Reissue with the Author's Final Revisions* (New York: Macmillan, 1961), p. 25; Graves, the lecture entitled "The White Goddess" (*OP*, p. 227).

59. *A Vision*, pp. 12, 8, 24–25. In a recent essay, James Olney has neatly synopsized the dynamics of Yeatsian skepticism; he speaks of "the assertion / denial, give-with-one-hand / take-away-with-the-other and always have-

it-both-ways strategy that Yeats practices whenever anything of the occult is in question." "W. B. Yeats's Daimonic Memory," *Sewanee Review* 85 (1977): 583–603 (595).

60. Mehoke, *Robert Graves: Peace-Weaver*, p. 102n.

61. Day, *Swifter than Reason*, p. 166.

62. *Fairy and Folk Tales of the Irish Peasantry*, ed. and selected by W. B. Yeats (London: Walter Scott, 1888), pp. 80, 146.

63. Ricks, *New Statesman* 68 (24 July 1964).

64. Spears, "The Latest Graves: Poet and Private Eye," p. 665. Mehoke, p. 161; Day, p. 166.

65. But, characteristically, Yeats goes on to note that his correspondent, the author of *Darkness My Bride*, is "not a 'materialist,' " and concludes, as though he himself were an orthodox mystical Christian: "I greet the lamb." *The Letters of W. B. Yeats*, ed. Allan Wade (London: Rupert Hart-Davis, 1954), p. 921.

66. Laura (Riding) Jackson, "Suitable Criticism," *University of Toronto Quarterly* 47 (Fall 1977), pp. 74–85 (81–82).

67. "Genius," in *Difficult Questions, Easy Answers* (New York: Doubleday, 1972), pp. 20, 21. In 1929, Graves's father-in-law, the artist William Nicholson, received a "postcard from Robert and Laura, to say that they are leaving for Spain together to *stop time*," a project related to Peter Quennell with a "dubious shake of the head." Quennell, "The Multiple Robert Graves," *Horizon* 4 (January 1962): 50–55 (53).

68. *WG*, p. 343. For Yeats's reading of Dunne, see his letter of 4 December 1931 to L. A. G. Strong (*Letters*, pp. 787–88).

69. "Genius," in *Difficult Questions, Easy Answers*, p. 21. Day (p. 105n) quotes Laura Riding's remarks from Stanley Kunitz, *Authors Today and Yesterday* (1933), p. 565.

70. In Graves's famous description of sexual love, "Exquisite in the pulse of tainted blood, / That *shivering glory* not to be despised," the italicized phrase (reminiscent of Herrick's "wild civility," Blake's "fearful symmetry," and Yeats's "terrible beauty"), specifically fuses, I would suggest, the "feathered glory" and the "shudder in the loins" of "Leda and the Swan," a Yeats poem Graves recalls elsewhere in describing "That horror with which Leda quaked / Under the spread wings of the swan." Predictably, Graves's "Leda" is (in its own word) the "beastliest" of the many poetic treatments of the Leda myth.

71. In *New Collected Poems*, the verb *charged* is misprinted as *changed*, an error that seriously distorts the passage.

72. Graves described himself at about this time (early fifties) in "The Face in the Mirror": "Grey haunted eyes . . . / Cheeks, furrowed; coarse grey hair, flying frenetic; / Forehead, wrinkled and high; / . . . Teeth, few. . . ."

73. Keats's last line—"Silent, upon a peak in Darien"—echoed also in "Mid-Winter Waking," may contribute to the description, here in "Darien," of the Goddess, who would "ascend the peak and pass from sight."

74. It is a strategy based on nature, which "abhors a straight line."

Graves quotes the axiom with approval and goes on to illustrate it, concluding by supplying the line breaks for the "unconscious burst of poetry" he once found in a Victorian mathematical textbook: "No lateral force, however great, / Can stretch a cord, however fine, / Into a horizontal line / That shall be absolutely straight" (*OP*, pp. 252–53).

75. The "most prideful" remark is taken from William H. Pritchard's favorable review of a recent volume of Graves's poetry in *The Hudson Review* 25 (Spring 1972); the other remark is from Robert Mazzocco's less admiring piece on Graves in *New York Review of Books* 4 (March 1965): 10.

76. Stade, *Robert Graves* (New York: Columbia University Press, 1967), p. 1. Bromwich, *Hudson Review* 30 (Summer 1977): 287.

77. "First and Last Romantics," *Studies in Romanticism* 9 (Fall 1970): 225–32 (230–31); later the opening essay in Bloom's *The Ringers in the Tower* (Chicago: University of Chicago Press, 1971).

78. "Advice on May Day," in *Poems and Satires 1951*.

79. For a more favorable account of Graves's employment of these techniques, see Robin Skelton, "Craft and Ceremony: Some Notes on the Versecraft of Robert Graves," in the *Malahat Review* symposium, pp. 37–48. The comment on Auden is John Bayley's, in *The Romantic Survival: A Study in Poetic Evolution* (London: Constable, 1957), p. 178.